INTRODUCTION TO THE
READING OF LACAN

THE LACANIAN CLINICAL FIELD

A series of books edited by
Judith Feher-Gurewich
in collaboration with Susan Fairfield

INTRODUCTION TO THE READING OF LACAN

The Unconscious Structured Like a Language

JOËL DOR

EDITED BY JUDITH FEHER-GUREWICH
IN COLLABORATION WITH SUSAN FAIRFIELD

OTHER

Other Press
New York

This work, published as part of the program of aid for publication, received support from the Ministry of Foreign Affairs of the Cultural Service of the French Embassy in the United States. *Cet ouvrage publié dans le cadre du programme d'aide à la publication bénéficie du soutien du Ministère des Affaires Etrangères du Service Culturel de l'Ambassade de France représenté aux Etats-Unis.*

Production Editor: Robert D. Hack

This book was set in 11 pt. Berkeley by Alpha Graphics of Pittsfield, New Hampshire.

2004 printing

10 9 8 7 6

Library of Congress Cataloging-in-Publication Data

Dor, Joël.
    [Introduction à la lecture de Lacan. English]
    Introduction to the reading of Lacan : the unconscious structured
like a language / by Joël Dor ; edited by Judith Feher-Gurewich
in collaboration with Susan Fairfield.
        p.   cm.
    Previously published : Paris : Denoël, c1985.
    Includes bibliographical references (p. 255) and index.
    ISBN 1-892746-04-2 (alk. paper)
    1. Psychoanalysis.   2. Lacan, Jacques, 1901–   .   I. Gurewich,
Judith Feher.   II. Fairfield, Susan.   III. Title
BF173.D55713   1997
150.19'5'092—dc20   96-17924

Contents

PART III
DESIRE—LANGUAGE—THE UNCONSCIOUS

The Lacanian Clinical Field:
Series Overview

Lacanian psychoanalysis exists, and the new series, The Lacanian Clinical Field, is here to prove it. The clinical expertise of French practitioners deeply influenced by the thought of Jacques Lacan has finally found a publishing home in the United States. Books that have been acclaimed in France, Italy, Spain, Greece, South America, and Japan for their clarity, didactic power, and clinical relevance will now be at the disposal of the American psychotherapeutic and academic communities. These books cover a range of topics, including theoretical introductions; clinical approaches to neurosis, perversion, and psychosis; child psychoanalysis; conceptualizations of femininity; psychoanalytic readings of American literature; and more. Thus far twelve books have been published.

Though all these works are clinically relevant, they will also be of great interest to those American scholars who have taught and used Lacan's theories for over a decade. What better opportunity for the academic world of literary criticism, philosophy, human sciences, women's studies, film studies, and multicultural studies finally to have access to the clinical insights of a theorist known primarily for his revolutionary vision of the formation of the human subject. Thus the Lacanian Clinical Field goes beyond introducing the American clinician to a different psychoanalytic outlook. It brings together two communities that have grown progressively estranged from each other. For indeed, the time when the Frankfurt School, Lionel Trilling, Erich Fromm, Herbert Marcuse, Philip Rieff, and others were fostering exchanges between the academic and the psychoanalytic communities is gone, and in the process psychoanalysis has lost some of its vibrancy.

The very limited success of ego psychology in bringing psychoanalysis into the domain of science has left psychoanalysis in need of a metapsychology that is able not only to withstand the pernicious challenges of psychopharmacology and psychiatry but also to accommodate the findings of cognitive and developmental psychology. Infant research has put many of Freud's insights into question, and the attempts to replace a one-body psychology with a more interpersonal or intersubjective approach have led to dissension within the psychoanalytic community. Many theorists are of the opinion that the road toward scientific legitimacy requires a certain allegiance with Freud's detractors, who are convinced that the unconscious and its sexual underpinnings are merely an aberration. Psychoanalysis continues to be practiced, however, and according to both patients and analysts the uncovering of unconscious motivations continues to provide a sense of relief. But while there has been a burgeoning of different psychoanalytic schools of thought since the desacralization of Freud, no theoretical agreement has been reached as to why such relief occurs.

Nowadays it can sometimes seem that Freud is read much more scrupulously by literary critics and social scientists than by psychoanalysts. This is not entirely a coincidence. While the psychoanalytic community is searching for a new meta-psychology, the human sciences have acquired a level of theoretical sophistication and complexity that has enabled them to read Freud under a new lens. Structural linguistics and structural anthropology have transformed conventional appraisals of human subjectivity and have given Freud's unconscious a new status. Lacan's teachings, along with the works of Foucault and Derrida, have been largely responsible for the explosion of new ideas that have enhanced the interdisciplinary movement pervasive in academia today.

The downside of this remarkable intellectual revolution, as far as psychoanalysis is concerned, is the fact that Lacan's contribution has been derailed from its original trajectory. No longer perceived as a theory meant to enlighten the practice of psychoanalysis, his brilliant formulations have been both adapted and criticized so as to conform to the needs of purely intellectual endeavors far removed from clinical reality. This state of affairs is certainly in part responsible for Lacan's dismissal by the psychoanalytic community. Moreover, Lacan's "impossible" style has been seen as yet another proof of the culture of obscurantism that French intellectuals seem so fond of.

In this context the works included in The Lacanian Clinical Field should serve as an eye-opener at both ends of the spectrum. The authors in the series are primarily clinicians eager to offer to professionals in psychoanalysis, psychiatry, psychology, and other mental health disciplines a clear and succinct didactic view of Lacan's work. Their goal is not so much to emphasize the radically new insights of the Lacanian theory of subjectivity and its place in the history of human sciences as it is to show how this difficult and complex body of ideas can enhance clinical work. Therefore, while the American clinician will be made aware that Lacanian psychoanalysis is not primarily a staple of literary criticism or philosophy but a praxis meant to cure patients of their psychic distress, the academic community will be exposed for the first time to a reading of Lacan that is in sharp contrast with the literature that has thus far informed them about his theory. In that sense Lacan's teachings return to the clinical reality to which they primarily belong.

Moreover, the clinical approach of the books in this series will shed a new light on the critical amendments that literary scholars and feminist theoreticians have brought to Lacan's conceptualization of subjectivity. While Lacan has been applauded for having offered an alternative to Freud's biological determinism, he has also been accused of nevertheless remaining phallocentric in his formulation of sexual difference. Yet this criticism, one that may be valid outside of the clinical reality—psychoanalysis is both an ingredient and an effect of culture—may not have the same relevance in the clinical context. For psychoanalysis as a praxis has a radically different function from the one it currently serves in academic discourse. In the latter, psychoanalysis is perceived both as an ideology fostering patriarchal beliefs and as a theoretical tool for constructing a vision of the subject no longer dependent on a phallocratic system. In the former, however, the issue of phallocracy loses its political impact. Psychoanalytic practice can only retroactively unravel the ways in which the patient's psychic life has been constituted, and in that sense it can only reveal the function the phallus plays in the psychic elaboration of sexual difference.

The Lacanian Clinical Field, therefore, aims to undo certain prejudices that have affected Lacan's reputation up to now in both the academic and the psychoanalytic communities. While these prejudices stem from rather different causes—Lacan is perceived as too patriarchal and reactionary in the one and too far removed from clinical reality in the other—they both seem to overlook the fact that the fifty years that cover the period of Lacan's teachings were mainly devoted to working and reworking the meaning and function of psychoanalysis, not necessarily as a science, or even as a human science, but as a practice that can nonetheless rely on a solid and coherent metapsychology. This double debunking of received notions may not only enlarge the respective frames of reference of both the therapeutic and the academic communities; it may also allow them to find a common denominator in a metapsychology that has derived its "scientific" status from the unexpected realm of the humanities.

I would like to end this overview to the series as a whole with a word of warning and a word of reassurance. One of the great difficulties for an American analyst trying to figure out the Lacanian "genre" is the way these clinical theorists explain their theoretical point of view as if it were coming straight from Freud. Yet Lacan's Freud and the American Freud are far from being transparent to each other. Lacan dismantled the Freudian corpus and rebuilt it on entirely new foundations, so that the new edifice no longer resembled the old. At the same time he always downplayed, with a certain *coquetterie*, his position as a theory builder, because he was intent on proving that he had remained, despite all odds, true to Freud's deepest insights. Since Lacan was very insistent on keeping Freudian concepts as the raw material of his theory, Lacanian analysts of the second generation have followed in their master's footsteps and have continued to read Freud scrupulously in order to expand, with new insights, this large structure that had been laid out. Moreover, complicated historical circumstances have fostered their isolation, so that their acquaintance with recent psychoanalytic developments outside of France has been limited. Lacan's critical views on ego psychology and selected aspects of object relations

theory have continued to inform their vision of American psychoanalysis and have left them unaware that certain of their
misgivings about these schools of thought are shared by some
of their colleagues in the United States. This apparently undy-
ing allegiance to Freud, therefore, does not necessarily mean that
Lacanians have not moved beyond him, but rather that their
approach is different from that of their American counterparts.
While the latter often tend to situate their work as a reaction to
Freud, the Lacanian strategy always consists in rescuing Freud's
insights and resituating them in a context free of biological determinism.

Second, I want to repeat that the expository style of the
books of this series bears no resemblance to Lacan's own writings. Lacan felt that Freud's clarity and didactic talent had ultimately led to distortions and oversimplifications, so that his own
notoriously "impossible" style was meant to serve as a metaphor
for the difficulty of listening to the unconscious. Cracking his
difficult writings involves not only the intellectual effort of readers but also their unconscious processes; comprehension will
dawn as reader-analysts recognize in their own work what
was expressed in sibylline fashion in the text. Some of Lacan's
followers continued this tradition, fearing that clear exposition
would leave no room for the active participation of the reader.
Others felt strongly that, although Lacan's point was well taken,
it was not necessary to prolong indefinitely an ideology of
obscurantism liable to fall into the same traps as the ones
Lacan was denouncing in the first place. Such a conviction was
precisely what made this series, The Lacanian Clinical Field,
possible.

—Judith Feher-Gurewich

Editor's Preface

JUDITH FEHER-GUREWICH

Introduction to the Reading of Lacan: The Unconscious Structured Like a Language, which inaugurates the series, was hailed by the French press. The journal *Psychologies* (May 1985) proclaimed it "an event" and praised the way in which Joël Dor proves that, contrary to what had been believed, Lacan's work can be made understandable, that it is possible to be simple and clear while staying close to the text. Furthermore, the review continued, Dor never confronts us with the aridity of too much theoretical presentation, since he illustrates his points with examples that bring together theory and its clinical applications. *Le Matin de Paris*, a daily newspaper, welcomed the volume on April 2, 1985 as a much-awaited reference book, an indispensable working tool both for clinicians eager to figure out Lacan's theory and for scholars in the various human sciences that Lacan's work draws upon. These reviews, among many others, led to a success that won this book a place on the nonfiction bestseller list.

Clearly, the hunger to understand Lacan in this country is far less pronounced than it is in France, where the Lacanian enigma had become almost a matter of national curiosity. Dor's

Introduction was geared toward an audience—primarily students and seasoned clinicians in the mental health disciplines, but also educated laypersons—that was eagerly awaiting the elucidation of ideas that they knew about without being able to make sense of them. Hence scholars in the human sciences will immediately discover in the Table of Contents the entries that concern one of their main interests, namely the link between structuralism, linguistic theory, and Lacan's famous formulation that the unconscious is structured like a language. American analysts, on the other hand, as they glance over the same Table of Contents, may resist this education in structural linguistics unless they know the clinical payoff of such forced labor. It may therefore be useful to state briefly the clinical relevance of some of the themes that are taken up in this book.

Part One: Linguistics and the Formation of the Unconscious is devoted to showing that Lacan's return to Freud through the detour of structural linguistics is neither farfetched nor antithetical to Freud's deepest insights. This is an important point, in that it demonstrates how the dream work and the formations of the unconscious operate according to laws that, to a certain extent, parallel those that are intrinsic to the structure of language. What Dor intends to show in this section is that principles that were later discovered by linguistic theory are already implicit in Freud's work. Lacan's contribution in this area is, therefore, to have pointed out and elaborated this remarkable convergence. The consequence of this link may not be immediately apparent; many chapters in this section will simply explain what is remarkable about Freud's own definitions of condensation and displacement, the joke, and the symptom, and about the way in which these formations of the unconscious reproduce certain tropes of rhetoric such as metaphor and metonymy or certain principles that regulate at a deeper level the actual structure of language per se.

Although clinical examples are offered that vividly illustrate the connection between the linguistic and the psychoanalytic realms, the clinical import of the linguistic tools will become more apparent further along. What Dor's demonstration brings to the fore at this point is a vision of the Freudian unconscious that cannot be described merely in terms of drive theory. The precision of a new human science, linguistics, offers insight into the old nature/nurture debate that psychoanalysis so far has not been able to resolve. In the Lacanian perspective, the unconscious occupies the space between nature and culture yet derives its mode of operation not from within but from without. What is not apparent to us when we speak—the functioning of language—is akin to what is not apparent to us when we desire through speech—the functioning of the unconscious. Even though the scientific "proof" of the unconscious cannot be arrived at according to positivistic principles, it remains the case that the "truth" of its functioning can at least be elucidated according to models that are no less rigorous.

The second and third parts of the book elucidate quite brilliantly the ways in which Lacan's theory of the birth of the human subject moves beyond Freud. The linguistic elements described in the previous section take on clinical relevance as they help to resituate Freud's Oedipus complex in the arena of intersubjectivity. Dor has succeeded in rearticulating in a logical sequence many insights that are spread throughout Lacan's work, but these sections also present his own original contribution, which consists in offering an alternative model to our common understanding of psychic development.

The oral, anal, and genital stages are reinscribed in a framework enriched by theorization of the mirror stage and of the child's acquisition of language in a process that Lacan equates with the acceptance of the incest taboo. In a back-and-forth movement between Lacan's formulations and Freud's texts, Dor breaks the Oedipus complex down into three phases in such a way as to link the mirror stage with the first phase, and the acquisition of language and the paternal metaphor with the second and third. This approach allows readers familiar with Freud's work to see for themselves Lacan's amendments and revisions to Freud's discoveries, in particular his very specific and interesting treatment of the phallus, which Dor explains with great clarity. What is unique in Dor's explanations, moreover (as many scholars who have struggled with Lacan's writings will promptly realize), is the way in which he illuminates clinical reality in his vivid descriptions of how human subjects are divided by the very processes that caused their existence, of how their alienation into language is revealed through the analytic process, and, ultimately, of how the unconscious is determined and structured through the signifiers of primordial Others.

While Part Two retraces the genesis of the human subject, Part Three concentrates on the "history of human desire." Here again specific texts of Freud, such as the "Project for a Scientific Psychology" of 1895, Chapter Seven of the Dream Book of 1900, and *Instincts and Their Vicissitudes* (1915), are brought together and recast in a new metapsychological perspective. How can we make sense of the problematic Freudian theory of the drives, when the only data that we can access as analysts are the discourse of the patient, his silences, his slips of the tongue, his jokes, his acting out, and the like? In order to formulate a theory of subjectivity that keeps alive Freud's insights without falling prey to biological determinism, it is necessary to retrace our steps backward from the discourse of the patient until we come to the point where the "traces" of the unconscious are no longer available. In other words, such a theory cannot claim to ground its formulation on a biological substrate.

Against this background, certain questions naturally arise. How can we distinguish need from human desire, when clinical reality seems to indicate that the satisfaction of the former rarely suffices to bring happiness to the patient? How can we understand the vicissitudes of human communication, when we realize that we seek in others precisely what others seek in ourselves, that is, recognition of our humanity beyond the objects that demand appears to designate? Joël Dor addresses these crucial issues by mapping out the trajectory of desire as it slides under the intentionality of conscious discourse. The graphs he uses to demonstrate the intricate relations between what we mean to communicate and how we are led, paradoxically, to miss our target provide a model of human interaction unmatched thus far in the psychoanalytic field. Having a grasp of these complex dynamics of desire will allow the reader to understand why it is that psychoanalysis brings about a sense of relief, in particular at those times when the patient comes to encounter what Lacan calls *full speech*, that is, a moment in the treatment when unconscious desire finds a way to articulate itself in discourse.

It is unquestionable that Dor's *Introduction to the Reading of Lacan* is an efficient book that systematically and forcefully presents the architectonics of Lacan's theory. However, the need of the American clinician to understand what a Lacanian analyst actually does in his practice is not addressed in Lacan's complex work. In order to fill this gap, the reader may next turn to the second volume in this series, *The Clinical Lacan*, as a companion text to the *Introduction*. Consisting of Joël Dor's lectures to psychoanalysts in training, this manual is centered on the diagnosis of psychic structure and thus provides immediate access to the landmarks that guide Lacanian psychoanalytic practice.

Introduction

JOËL DOR

The *Introduction to the Reading of Lacan* reviews the main arguments developed in a series of talks held outside the circles in which the teaching of psychoanalysis is usually welcome—universities and psychoanalytic or psychiatric institutes. This "outside" had to have an address in order that, from 1981 on, an approach to the work of Lacan could be painstakingly outlined for an audience, and the actual location helped to identify this approach symbolically as the Seminar of the Music Room. But as advantageous as this autonomy was at first because of the circumstances in which psychoanalysis found itself at the time, it was eventually necessary to have an institutional home in which instruction could continue permanently. This was the Centre de Formation et de Recherches Psychanalytiques (Center for Psychoanalytic Training and Research).

From the beginning, the project of instruction had to be negotiated as a wager. It was offered to an audience of clinicians in training (psychologists, psychiatrists, analysts), who had in common not only their failure to understand Lacan, but also their lively desire to start working to overcome this ignorance.

It was important, therefore, to develop and make available a course of instruction that was strongly didactic. That seemed to be all that was required to achieve the goal of *introducing* the audience to the *reading* of a body of psychoanalytic work reputed to be difficult. But this pedagogical concern was no reason to sacrifice the integrity of the work we were undertaking in favor of oversimplifications or rhetorical clarifications. Instead of looking out for the elegance of the exposition or the style of the commentary, it was more appropriate to maintain the consistency and the internal logic of Lacan's work down to its smallest esoteric details, even at the price of an argument that was sometimes dry and full of twists and turns. Thus, in setting forth these arguments, there was no obliging routine of meaningful winks, no gratifying of any preference for verbose oracular pathos or abstruse jargon. There was, at most, a constant vigilance with regard to this massive and complex body of work, a strategy of approach that would allow it to be explored methodically in its major peaks and essential ravines.

With this in mind, it was clear that the *return to Freud* was the best way to lay the groundwork for the basic formulation of Lacan's thought. This involved using the Freudian corpus to define key elements of the most crucial Lacanian concepts as well as their integration into the development of Lacan's first theoretical statements. And it also involved relying on Freud's clinical writings as the primary source to which one had to return in order to illustrate the heuristic nature of these theories.

But beyond this allegiance to Freud, it was necessary to organize the exposition into a progressively developing argument. This coherence was assured thanks to a guiding statement, *the unconscious is structured like a language*, which was adopted as a working hypothesis directing the course of instruction and establishing its underlying goal: to justify this hypothesis fully.

Demonstrating that the unconscious is structured like a language was to a large extent a pedagogical device. But it was also well suited to the investigation of the fundamental principles of Lacan's work, since they are articulated most coherently in this way. Moreover, this methodology easily lent itself to selective digressions into a number of allied disciplines: brief references to basic tenets of structuralism, Saussurian linguistics, and Hegelian philosophy made it possible to illuminate as well as to support some of these theoretical advances.

With a similar view toward clarification, some diagrams and symbolic formulas were presented. These, taken together with Lacan's algorithms, should not in any way be thought to suggest the birth pangs of the "mathemes,"[1] or some process of formalization that was underway. At most, there was an attempt to find some arbitrary expedients to "metaphorize" in a concise way theoretical arguments that could sometimes seem too abstract.

In more general terms, the development of this course of instruction also had to adhere to some guiding—some would say ethical—choices in order to judge Lacan's thought appropriately. First, it was necessary to demystify the reputation of a body of work to which nonspecialists still often objected on the grounds that it was a totally hermetic compendium, esoteric and inaccessible to some beginning clinicians. Such fantasies were strongly confirmed by the myth of the theoretical treasure buried in the works of Lacan that had not yet been edited.[2] It was

---

1. Translator's note: "Mathemes" are mathematical formalizations devised by Lacan with the aim of making psychoanalytic theory more rigorous and precise.

2. On the published and unpublished work of Lacan see Dor 1984. The present study makes occasional reference to Lacan's unpublished seminars; these are taken from transcriptions of notes made during the seminars themselves or from shorthand records. There has been considerable controversy

also important to disband the initiatory cult of Lacan worship-
pers, in which certain ideas, removed from their theoretical
context, are eruditely deployed to adorn drab scholastic perora-
tions or wildly brandished like an interpretative cleaver. Finally,
I wanted to contribute certain materials—though they are elementary, they can lead to cautious or beneficial revisions—to
the star performers of citation and to the veteran warriors of the
Lacanian maxim who are their allies in the debased usage of
formulas.

This course of instruction, however, could not stand by such
choices unless it were mindful of the emphasis Lacan constantly
placed on the effect of logical time. So it is important, in ap-
proaching his work, not to let the "time for understanding"
encroach on the "moment of the gaze"; nor, *a fortiori*, should
the "moment of concluding" encroach on the "time for understanding." Observing this logical imperative entails a presentation of Lacan's work that moves ahead at a moderate yet decisive pace, making sure that the initial arguments, at any rate,
have been brought together. On the other hand, to make way
for the challenging of basic principles or for misleading commentary would be to compromise a methodical introduction to
the work of Lacan, and without such an introduction any dispute risks discrediting itself in advance. Yet the circumscribed
range of this didactic presentation only makes it all the more
clear that interrogation of the work itself, a work clearly open
to criticism, must be put off until a later time.

---

about the "fidelity" of these documents of different origin and varying quality. One such transcription, called "the version of the secretariat" because it
is supposed to have been officially approved by Lacan, is viewed as more re-
liable and is the basis of my references here pending the official edition of the
texts.

Insofar as interrogation would presuppose that the "time for understanding" had already come about, there could not, paradoxically, be any form of closure at the end of this course of instruction other than the suspension of the "moment of concluding." This deliberate absence of a conclusion has a double justification.

First, it was appropriate to end at just the right point of the work being studied to accomplish the original aim of this presentation: to be an *introduction* to the *reading*. It became obvious that going ahead without delay in this reading was in itself a sensible way to conclude.

Second, it was also necessary to take the exact measure of the progress made in this present approach, essentially devoted to the basic formulations of Lacan's work. Not to conclude this *Introduction* was, therefore, to opt for undertaking a sequel that would clarify, at whatever length was justified, the subsequent development of the work that had been begun. Discerning the conceptual modification of certain initial theoretical fragments, introducing the establishment of new arguments; my current teaching activity is being pursued with such a sequel in mind.[3]

Sticking to the requirement for a didactic presentation would seem, from many sides, to contradict Lacan's repeated warning against "the inanity of the discourse of knowledge," the prime example of which he saw in "the workings of university discourse when it sets forth this fiction that it calls an author" (Lemaire 1977, p. 6). But at least we can bet that the use of didactic discourse to set forth an author in written form will facilitate access to the work of an author who is, as a result, fictive.

---

3. Translator's note: The sequel, *Introduction à la lecture de Lacan, 2: La structure du sujet*, was published by Denoël, Paris, 1992.

The "Return to Freud"

An introduction to Lacan's work should define the principal articulations of his theory through an approach that may be preliminary, but is neither elementary nor schematic. What is most important is to mark out the terrain from which Lacan himself set forth. This is the Freudian terrain, the *Freudian field*, on both the practical and theoretical levels, and it is the infrastructure of Lacan's theoretical architectonics throughout his work.

This Freudian reference is above all a reference to a certain way of understanding the unconscious. At the same time, it indicates a rigorously codified practice based on a principle of investigation whose fundamental originality is unmistakable. Thus we have to define from the outset what belongs to authentic psychoanalytic practice as opposed to other procedures for the investigation of the unconscious—procedures that, while they may claim to be derived from psychoanalysis, have completely lost touch with its meaning.

The Freudian investigation of the unconscious is marked by a certain psychic "seal" that assures us that we are not dealing with an abstract or metaphysical entity. Nor are we in the register of a biological entity or of some measurable and quantifiable psychic substrate. In the very principle underlying their discovery, the unconscious processes described by Freud are dependent on the psychic dimension of language and on the fulcrums that sustain it in the transference.

There are, then, two poles, language and the transference, that are the organizing principles of the practice authentically inaugurated by Freud. Nonetheless, it must be noted that although analytic practice is a practice of language, all practices of language are not necessarily psychoanalytic. Moreover, if the essential articulation of the unconscious is in speech, we may wonder about the aspect of misrecognition on the part of certain practices that claim to be psychoanalytically based but that have broken all ties with language.

Lacan made no concessions as far as these radical distinctions are concerned, if only because the second pole, the transference, pins down the Freudian unconscious and the practice that derives from it. The dimension of transference requires all the more attention, given Freud's aphorism, "Wherever there is transference, there is psychoanalysis." But does this mean that the establishment of a transference is enough to qualify a practice as authentically psychoanalytic? Some supplementary comments are necessary for the full understanding of Freud's words. As soon as one subject speaks to another, there is transference. ("In its essence the efficacious transference which we're considering is quite simply the speech act. Each time a man speaks to another in an authentic and full manner there is, in the true sense, transference, symbolic transference—something takes place which changes the nature of the two beings present" [Lacan 1953–1954, p. 109].) But if a transference may develop out of any encounter, all the conditions for a certain *manipulation of the transference* are therefore implicitly present in that encounter. What radically separates analytic practice in the Freudian sense from other practices that may wrongly claim kinship with psychoanalysis is the fate reserved for the dimension of transference. Any encounter with a supposedly therapeutic goal can easily develop in a register of manipulation of the transference. Analytic practice, on the other hand, can be established only in a frame in which any attempt at manipulation of the transference is neutralized. Psychoanalytic practice unfolds in the register of the *analysis of the transference*: it is in this operative space that the patient is called upon to investigate his own unconscious, and hence it is in this space that he will most surely be confronted by the question of his desire.

This is but a reminder of a few very general aspects of the Freudian reference to the unconscious and the practice on which it is based. It is this sort of commonplace, however, that the first generations of analysts sometimes misunderstood without realizing it. What happened was that the basic requirements for the experience of the unconscious soon underwent compromises and adaptations. One of Lacan's constant preoccupations was to restore the Freudian originality of the experience of the unconscious under the banner of a daring hypothesis: *the unconscious is structured like a language*. We may even consider this to be the most fundamental hypothesis in all of Lacan's theoretical work, if only because it both presupposes and embodies the meaning of the *return to Freud* that Lacan ceaselessly advocated throughout his career.

Lacan first announced this *return to Freud* in the "Rome Discourse" of 1953. (The complete title is "Function and field of speech and language in psychoanalysis" [Lacan 1953b].) The full

implications of what he had to say here must be seen in the light
of the schism within the French psychoanalytic movement in
that year. In his preface, Lacan specifies what is at stake:

> Before proceeding to the report itself, something should be
> said of the surrounding circumstances. For they had some
> effect on it.
>
> The theme was suggested to the author as the basis of
> the customary theoretical report for the annual meeting of
> the society, which, at that time, represented psychoanalysis
> in France. For eighteen years, this society had pursued what
> had become a venerable tradition under the title "Congrès
> des Psychanalystes de langue française," then for two years
> this congress had been extended to psychoanalysts speak-
> ing any of the Romance languages (Holland being included
> out of linguistic tolerance). The Congress in question took
> place in Rome in September [1953].
>
> Meanwhile, serious disagreements led to a secession in
> the French group. These disagreements came to a head on
> the occasion of the foundation of an "institute of psycho-
> analysis." The group that had succeeded in imposing its stat-
> utes and programme on the new institute was then heard to
> declare that it would prevent the members who, with oth-
> ers, had tried to introduce a different conception into the
> institute, from speaking at Rome, and it tried every means
> in its power to do so. [Lacan 1953b, p. 30]

The "different conception" of which Lacan was accused was
precisely his argument defending the necessity for a return to
Freud. The "urgent task" was "to disengage from concepts that
are being deadened by routine use the meaning that they regain
both from a re-examination of their history and from a reflexion
on their subjective foundations" (p. 33). To formulate it differently, Lacan was concerned to denounce "the temptation for the

analyst to abandon the foundation of speech" (p. 36). It is here that Lacan (1955) specifies that "the meaning of a return to Freud is a return to the meaning of Freud" (p. 117) or the return to the order of the "Freudian Thing." A psychoanalyst, he reminds us, "should find it easy enough to grasp the fundamental distinction between signifier and signified, and to begin to use the two non-overlapping networks of relations that they organize" (p. 126).

In his commentary on the "Situation of psychoanalysis in 1956," Lacan (1956) repeated his emphasis on shifting the focus back to the dimension of the symbolic that Freud had defined on the basis of his experience of the unconscious:

> To know what happens in analysis we must know where speech comes from. To know what resistance is, we must know what forms a screen against the advent of speech. . . .
> Why evade the questions that the unconscious brings up?
> If so-called "free" association gives us access [to the unconscious], is it by means of a release comparable to those of neurobiological automatisms?
> If the drives discovered [in the unconscious] are on the diencephalic or even the rhinencephalic level, how can we understand them as structured in terms of language?
> For if, from the very start, it is in language that [the drives] make known their effects, then their subterfuges, which we have come to recognize, denote, no less in their triviality than in their refinement, a linguistic procedure. [pp. 461, 466]

Following the example of Freud, who had included the range of philological studies in the program of an ideal psychoanalytic training institute, Lacan (1956) prescribed the rudiments of linguistics to analysts in training. The essential notion was "the distinction between the signifier and the signified, for

which we rightly honor Ferdinand de Saussure, since it is
through his teachings that this distinction has now become fundamental to the humanities" (p. 467).

From 1956 on, Lacan stressed the notion of the "primacy
of the signifier over the signified," considering it to be one of
the most obvious consequences of the *Interpretation of Dreams*.

> The dream is a rebus (says Freud). He did not have to elaborate on this for us to understand that he was referring to the
> words of the soul. Have the phrases of a rebus ever made the
> least bit of sense, and the interest we have in deciphering it,
> doesn't it come from the fact that the meaning manifested
> in its images is annulled, having no relevance except to make
> intelligible the disguised signifier? [Lacan 1956, p. 470]

Lacan describes the way that, from the outset, the subject
is captured by this primacy of the signifier, specifically by the
alienation that he fosters with his symptoms. The meaning
of the symptoms, as it emerges in the analytic context, is such
that it confirms the idea that "the technique of psychoanalysis,
working with the relation of the subject to the signifier, has
gained only the knowledge that is organized around this relation" (Lacan 1956, p. 472).

But it was in 1957 that Lacan gave his decisive definition
of the impact of this return to Freud, the essence of which is
directly connected to the notion of language. This is the theme
of his authoritative lecture, "The agency of the letter in the unconscious or reason since Freud" (Lacan 1957a), where his innovative meaning is made clear right in the opening remarks:

> And how could a psychoanalyst of today not realize that
> speech is the key to that truth, when his whole experience
> must find in speech alone its instrument, its context, its

material, and even the background noise of its uncertainties.
. . . As my title suggests, beyond this "speech," what the psychoanalytic experience discovers in the unconscious is the
whole structure of language. [p. 147]

An introduction to Lacan must establish the basis for all the
details of the proposition that the unconscious is structured like
a language. It is necessary, first of all, to look into Freud's work
for evidence of this principle and of its relevance. Since *The Interpretation of Dreams* is considered Freud's master text, we will
use some of its central arguments to develop this justification.

We must remember that Freud's brilliant hypothesis about
dreams involves applying to them the same exploratory technique that he had successfully applied to psychological manifestations such as obsessions and anxiety: the *method of free
association*. This technique was favored because of the inade-
quacies and impasses encountered in the use of the hypnotic and
cathartic methods. Free association made it possible to identify
the meaning of psychic manifestations originating in the unconscious. Because of its operative properties, it also led to the notion
of an unconscious *formation*—in other words, to the generalization of a multiplicity of psychic manifestations that all have
in common the characteristic of signifying something completely
different from what they seem to signify at first.

In the course of Freud's meticulous analysis of the "Dream
of Irma's injection" (Freud 1900), an idea takes form: the dream
is a discourse that is disguised, distorted, or condensed; the
subject has lost the code to decipher it, but the secret of its
strangeness is delivered up in a clear and meaningful form
through arduous associative work. In this respect, Freud from
the very start interrogates the dream, like other formations of
the unconscious, with reference to a system of signifying ele-

ments analogous to the signifying elements of language. He recalls us time and again to this order of language, since the investigation of the unconscious is always suspended in the flux of associative chains, and these, being nothing less than chains of thoughts, keep bringing us back to chains of words. In consequence, any hope of contenting ourselves with a pre-codified index of meanings, a key to the deciphering of dreams, must be abandoned. Even if Freud, as we know, attaches importance to symbols and symbolism in dreams, his dream theory in no way authorizes neglect of the subject's speech when it comes to the revelation of the unconscious. Here lies a decisive argument for Lacan's return to Freud: his project is to bring this dimension of speech back to the forefront of the psychoanalytic field.

We also find here the outline of another basic idea that Lacan took from Freud concerning one of the most fundamental properties of the unconscious: the subject cannot make himself understood by any signifying element that can be predicted in advance. As we continue to identify the fundamental points of Lacan's thought, we may note that, beyond Freud's distinction between latent and manifest content in dreams, the intuition takes form that a discourse always says more than it anticipates saying, beginning with the fact that it can mean something completely different from what is at first uttered. Lacan extends this referential entanglement of the unconscious in the net of discourse to its most extreme consequences, even to the point of seeing it as a property inevitably brought about by the structure of the speaking subject.

Part I

Linguistics and the Formation of the Unconscious

2

Condensation and Displacement in Dream Work

The primary Lacanian concepts behind the hypothesis that the unconscious is structured like a language are rooted in the Freudian theory of the dream. The most important notion here is that of the *dream work* (Freud 1900), which is directly based on the functioning of the various unconscious mechanisms of the primary process.

The dream work mainly involves two fundamental mechanisms: *condensation* and *displacement*. Empirical observation made Freud aware of the active presence of these two mechanisms; essentially what he perceived was the difference in "volume" between the manifest material and the latent dream thoughts, and the need to disguise the meaning of these latent thoughts.

In this way he came to distinguish several paradigms of condensation. First, there is condensation by *omission*. An excellent example occurs in the analysis of the "Dream of the Botanical Monograph" (Freud 1900), in which the reconstruction of the latent thoughts is very incomplete at the level of the manifest content. Another form of condensation consists of *fusion* or *superimposition* of the latent material. The most spectacular example of this is the elaboration of *composite persons* or the creation of *neologisms* by successive combinations and fusions. Irma, for example, is a composite character who represents a whole series of people who had been "sacrificed to the work of condensation" (p. 293). Similar instances are the "propyls" of the "Dream of Irma's Injection" (pp. 293–294) and the "positively norekdal style" (p. 296) in another of Freud's dreams. The obsessive childhood dream of the Wolf Man (Freud 1918) is also a stereotypical example of the process of condensation in the dream work.

The modifications that take place, during the dream work, in the passage from the content of the latent thoughts to the manifest content do not depend solely on the different processes of condensation. Latent ideas may be represented on the level of the manifest content after having undergone a major shift that Freud calls the reversal of values or of meaning. In other words, the dream work initiates a process of *displacement*, whose role is essentially to obscure, on the manifest level, what was fundamentally significant in the latent thoughts.

> It thus seems plausible to suppose that in the dream-work a psychical force is operating which on the one hand strips the elements which have a high psychical value of their intensity, and on the other hand, *by means of overdetermination*, creates from elements of low psychical value new values, which afterwards find their way into the dream-content. If that is so, *a transference and displacement of psychical intensities* occurs in the process of dream-formation, and it is as a result of these that the difference between the text of the dream-content and that of the dream-thoughts comes about. The process which we are here presuming is nothing less

than the essential portion of the dream-work; and it deserves to be described as "dream displacement." [Freud 1900, pp. 307–308; emphasis in original]

These are the principal elements—briefly summarized—of Freud's theory of dreams that Lacan uses to establish and to support his analogy between the mode of functioning of unconscious processes and that of certain aspects of language. But this idea, fundamental to the development of Lacanian theory, can be maintained only in the context of a structural conception of language. This structural perspective, originating in the work of Ferdinand de Saussure, will be examined later. But first a digression into the larger area of structuralist principles is in order, for at least two reasons: first, because the reference to structuralism underlies all of Lacan's theory, modifying its direction and its implications[1]; second, because the current use of the term *structure* is too often incorrect, revealing a misunderstanding of the denotations and connotations of a concept whose foundations were rigorously defined.

---

1. Lacan often made a point of saying that he was doing not linguistics, properly speaking, but "linguistry" (*linguisterie*). On Lacan's "linguistry" see the excellent article by N. Kress-Rosen (1981).

3

The Notion of Structure

The structuralist position is a strategy for promoting a new intelligibility, one that breaks with certain ways of thinking about objects. This change has been particularly fruitful in certain areas, though we must not overestimate its efficacy.

Structuralism opened up new horizons in the exact sciences and in the humanities because it was able to reveal that elements or objects were related according to systems that were not immediately apparent. This approach requires us to turn away, temporarily, from a certain mode of relating to objects; we must give up a certain type of description of their nature, qualities, and specific properties. What is important is to be receptive to the possibility of bringing to light hidden relations among objects or among their elements. This of course presupposes that we establish a certain coherence in the type of objects under consideration. These objects must fall within a similar designation or belong to a similar grouping. This is the necessary condition for the emergence of new principles of relation. These relations may be of different types: they may contrast these objects, differentiate them, transform them, animate them, and so on. They are the laws established among objects or their elements, laws that can reveal properties allowing us to determine a *structure* peculiar to the set of objects or elements under study.

We can immediately see the possible consequences of this new epistemological approach. First, it allows us to jettison the "compartmentalist" principal of analysis within a given discipline. Second, arbitrary partitioning between the various fields of study in a single discipline is deferred. For example, the implications of this strategy can be assessed right away in the field of mathematics, with the removal of the compartmentalization separating algebra, numerical analysis, geometry, probability theory, and the like; in psychology the atomistic carving up of psychic space can be abandoned; in linguistics diachronic segmentation is set aside; and so on.

Let us look at the development of a structure using an example from mathematics. The nineteenth-century mathematician Evariste Galois developed the concept of one of the most elementary structures, that of a group. According to Bourbaki, group structure is defined as follows: for a set G, we may say that an internal law of composition that is defined throughout determines a group structure if it is associative, if it has a neutral element, and if every element of G has a symmetric one.

Therefore, for the structure to exist we need not only a set of elements, but also a law that operates on them. To do this, the law must work under the following conditions:

1. First, the combination of two of the elements of the set must always constitute an element of the set:

$$E * E \rightarrow E$$
$$2 + 3 = 5$$

These are illustrations of an *internal rule*.

2. Next, the combination of several elements must be possible from any place in the sequence:

$$(a * b) * c = a * (b * c)$$

This is an *associative rule*.

3. Next, the set of elements must contain one that can be designated as neutral, such that, when it is combined with any other element in the set, it leaves that element identical to itself:

$$\begin{cases} \exists\, e \in E \\ e * a = a \end{cases}$$

For multiplication, the neutral element is $1 : 1 \cdot x = x$
For addition, the neutral element is $0 : 0 + 4 = 4$

4. Finally, there must exist for each element a symmetric element such that their combination equals the neutral element:

$$a * a' = e$$
$$3 \times \frac{1}{3} = 1$$
$$2 + (-2) = 0$$

This group structure remains valid whatever the nature of the mathematical elements chosen. Thus these elements may be numbers; geometrical elements such as vectors; analytic or vectorial functions; and so on. Under these conditions, one may define very general universes of objects, such as the group of relative integers, the group of affine transformations, the group of homothetic transformations, or the group of similarities. What these universes of objects have in common is the same group structure in relation to a specific law that combines their elements.

Going beyond this example, it is easy to understand in a general way the epistemological interest of the structuralist aim. The structural approach is a heuristic one that proceeds by *inclusive generalization*. A good example of this inclusive generalization (though it is not, strictly speaking, a structuralist strategy) is the discovery of non-Euclidean geometries in the nineteenth century. The work of Bolyaï, Lobachevski, and Riemann reveals systems that are more general than Euclid's geometry, but these more general aspects by no means invalidate Euclidean geometry, which becomes a *specific case* of a larger geometrical system that includes it.

If we can say that the structuralist attitude functions in somewhat the same way, it is because it leads to an inclusive generalization among structures themselves. There is, therefore, a hierarchy of structures, in the sense that certain stronger structures are able to subsume weaker ones. Thus vast systems of formalization can be organized, opening up new horizons of study. In conclusion, let us examine Jean Piaget's (1970) definition of the term "structure":

> A structure is a system of transformations. Inasmuch as it is a system and not a mere collection of elements and their properties, these transformations involve laws: the structure is preserved and enriched by the interplay of its transformation laws, which never yield results external to the system nor employ elements that are external to it. In short, the notion of structure is comprised of three key ideas: the idea of wholeness, the idea of transformation, and the idea of self-regulation. [p. 5]

According to Piaget, the *totality* is the result of both the interdependence of the elements composing the structures and the fact that the bringing together of all the elements is necessarily different from their sum. The notion of *transformation* presupposes laws of combination defining operations within a given structure in such a way that they, as it were, give structure to an already structured reality. Finally, *self-regulation*, the essential characteristic of the structure, means that the structure is self-preservative. For example, if two elements of a structure are brought into connection by the law of combination, the third element resulting from this operation will also be structured. In other words, one may speak of the *stability* of the system. Such a definition of structure is particularly suitable for the study of language. By way of illustration, we may briefly review certain aspects of the work of Ferdinand de Saussure that have influenced the primary elements of the connection Lacan establishes between language and the unconscious.

4

Elements of Structural Linguistics

The structuralist point of view in linguistics appeared with the introduction of the *synchronic dimension* in the study of language. We owe to Ferdinand de Saussure the discovery that this study cannot be reduced to a purely diachronic, that is to say historical, perspective. For in point of fact, the history of a word does not allow for an account of its present meaning, since this meaning depends on the *system* of the language to which it belongs. This system lies in certain laws of equilibrium that are directly dependent on synchrony. Moreover, there is a fundamental relation between meaning and signs that can be appreciated only from the synchronic point of view.

The synchronic perspective introduced by Saussure (1966) characterizes an approach that is specifically operative in the linguistic field, since the structural view reveals radically new properties of language. But this new perspective on linguistics has spread to other areas of the human sciences, providing an exceptionally fertile source for their renewal. Lacan applies the structuralist strategy to the field of psychoanalysis by introducing a number of principles borrowed from structural linguistics into psychoanalytic theory. These principles effect a radical epistemological change at the level of metapsychology.

Beginning with the Rome Discourse (1953b), Lacan resituates the problematics of the unconscious in a network of intelligibility based on the precepts of structural linguistics. This excerpt pinpoints the main elements of his thought:

> Take up the work of Freud again at the *Traumdeutung* [*Interpretation of Dreams*] to remind yourself that the dream has the structure of a sentence, or, rather, to stick to the letter of the work, of a rebus; that is to say, it has the structure of a form of writing, of which the child's dream represents the primordial ideography, and which, in the adult, reproduces the simultaneously phonetic and symbolic use of signifying elements, which can also be found both in the hieroglyphs of ancient Egypt and in the characters still used in China.
>
> But even this is no more than the deciphering of the instrument. The important part begins with the translation of the text, the important part that Freud tells us is given in the elaboration of the dream—that is to say, in its rhetoric. Ellipsis and pleonasm, hyperbaton or syllepsis, regression, repetition, apposition—these are the syntactical displacements; metaphor, catachresis, antonomasia, allegory, metonymy, and synecdoche—these are the semantic condensations in which Freud teaches us to read the ostentatious intentions, or the dissimulating, persuasive, retaliatory, or seductive demonstrations, out of which the subject models his oneiric discourse.
> [pp. 57–58, translation modified]

Lacan's elegantly invoked array of discursive tropes should not lead us to think that the analogy stops with dream discourse.

All the formations of the unconscious, without exception, come under the same heading:

> In the case of the psychopathology of everyday life, another field to which Freud dedicated one of his works, it is clear that every unsuccessful act is a sucessful, not to say "well turned," discourse, and that in the slip of the tongue it is the gag that hinges on speech, and exactly in the right quarter for its word to be sufficient to the wise. [Lacan 1953b, p. 58, translation modified]

It therefore seemed clear to Lacan that Freud's own work called for the introduction of certain concepts from linguistics into the field of psychoanalytic theory. But it is nonetheless true that, although Lacan worked tirelessly to mine this new vein, it had been hinted at as early as 1937 by the analyst Ella Freeman Sharpe (1961) in her *Dream Analysis*. Lacan's originality lies in formulating this intuition into a theory and raising it to the level of a general hypothesis concerning the unconscious. This is why the *structural analogy* between certain processes of language and the dynamics of the unconscious presupposes an acquaintance with linguistics. In fact, the notion of structure is central to Lacan's work only because of his frequent references to the structure of language: first, insofar as it is this very structure that Lacan posits as related to the unconscious, and second, because it is in the act of language that the unconscious emerges and finds its locus of expression. This analogy becomes clearer once we have examined two fundamental principles of Saussurian linguistics: the radical distinction between signifier and signified, and the differentiation between the two axes of language. What follows is a brief discussion of these two principles.

THE LINGUISTIC SIGN

The structural algorithm of language developed by Saussure (1966) at the beginning of this century is based first of all on the notion of the *linguistic sign*. To establish the nature of this sign, Saussure had to break with certain traditions of thought, in particular with the intuitively plausible idea that the linguistic unit is the association of a term with a thing. For in fact "the linguistic sign unites, not a thing and a name, but a concept and a sound-image" (p. 66). But what do we mean by "sound image"? According to Saussure, it is "not the material sound, a purely physical thing, but the psychological imprint of the sound, the impression that it makes on our senses. The sound-image is sensory, and if I happen to call it 'material,' it is only in that sense, and by way of opposing it to the other term of the association, the concept, which is generally more abstract" (p. 66).

We must take note of expressions like *psychological imprint* and *impression* that prefigure the fundamental distinction among *le langage, la langue* [both translated as "language" in English], and *parole* ["speech"]. As "psychic" entities, linguistic units belong in the register of *la langue* and are not a product of speech. It is for this reason that *langage* is seen as the utilization, the actual articulation, of a *langue* as spoken by a subject. As Saussure says, "for us, *langue* is *langage* minus *parole*" ["Language is speech minus speaking"] (p. 77). The linguistic sign thus appears as a "psychic entity with two sides," whose two components are established from the beginning in an *associative relation*. If the linguistic sign, then, is first and foremost a relation, this relation, which appears to be stable in the system of *la langue*, is susceptible to changes in the dimension of *langage*. Moreover, while Saussure retains the term "sign" to denote the linguistic unit, he substitutes "signified" for the concept and "signifier" for the acoustic image. ("I propose to retain the word *sign* [*signe*] to designate the whole and to replace *concept* and *sound-image* respectively by *signified* [*signifié*] and *signifier* [*signifiant*]; these last two terms have the advantage of indicating the opposition that separates them from each other and from the whole of which they are parts" [p. 67].) The sign then becomes the relation of a signifier to a signified that we can diagram in the following way:

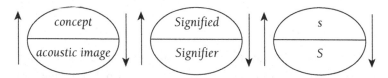

This is a relation of opposition separating the elements involved. It reveals a property of the sign that Lacan puts to use— *the autonomy of the signifier in relation to the signified*. This autonomy is possible only if the signifier and the signified are not in a fixed relation.

If we consider the linguistic sign to be the fundamental element in a language system, a brief examination of the way it functions in the system immediately reveals properties that may seem to be contradictory. These properties, which we will examine one by one, are the following: (1) the arbitrary nature of the sign; (2) the immutability of the sign; (3) the alteration of the sign; and (4) the linear nature of the signifier.

The Arbitrary Nature of the Sign

The arbitrariness of the sign appears at the level of the association between the signifier and the signified. In point of fact, no necessary connection exists between a concept and the acoustic image representing it. Proof of this is that the acoustic image for a given signified varies from one language to another. Nonetheless, the arbitrariness of the sign does not mean that it is aleatory by nature, since this arbitrariness is relevant only for a particular linguistic community: "The word arbitrary . . . should not imply that the choice of signifier depends entirely on the speaker. . . . I mean that it is unmotivated, i.e., arbitrary in that it actually has no natural connection with the signified" (pp. 68–69).

Clinical Remarks

The problem of the aleatory nature of the linguistic sign comes up in clinical situations such as certain delusional languages and psychopathological glossolalias, to give only two examples. It is mainly (but not exclusively) in cases of schizophrenia that we encounter severe language disorders in which the delusional structuring of speech points up exactly this difference between the sign's arbitrary nature and its aleatory nature. Though we must keep in mind Freud's (1915b) observation that in schizophrenia word presentations function as thing presentations, Saussure's theory of the linguistic sign allows us to clarify how matters stand with this aleatory type of association between a signifier and a signified. This mechanism of disconnecting signifier and signified leads Lacan to speak of the *unchaining of the signifier*. What may appear as unchaining of the signifier is the effect of a specific modification of the use of the linguistic sign, when, as Saussure puts it, "the choice of signifier is left entirely to the speaker" (p. 69).

This aleatory property of the elaboration and use of the linguistic sign has been especially well described in a paper by Serge Leclaire (1958). Leclaire demonstrates how two processes may be at work in the alteration of the sign: either a single signified may be associated with any signifier, or, inversely, a single signifier may be associated with any signified.

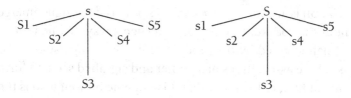

In both cases we end up with a strictly individual and subjective arbitrariness of the sign that is therefore no longer the
arbitrariness proper to a linguistic community. To the extent that
the arbitrariness here is specific and limited to a speaking subject, it may be said that the association of signifier and signified
is left completely open to aleatory possibilities of combination.
It is, of course, necessary to examine carefully the question of
unconscious overdetermination in signifying material combined
in this way, and a major part of Lacan's thinking addresses this
question.

But to return to the case of the psychopathological language
disorders known as glossolalias, the influence of unconscious
processes on the modification of the linguistic sign is perfectly
clear in spite of the apparently aleatory nature of the associations between signifiers and signifieds (see Dor 1982).

We may briefly define glossolalia as the ability to invent and
speak new languages that are completely incomprehensible to
everyone but the speaker. These original linguistic constructions
have a syntactic structure, more or less rudimentary, that is almost always analogous to that of the speaker's mother tongue.
In a certain number of cases these relatively structured languages
stabilize and become progressively richer. Such stability is essentially due to a certain fixity in the association of signifier and
signified, which, however, is by no means the result of an arbitrariness that is conventionally established and accepted by the
usage of a linguistic community. In glossolalia the process of

association is aleatory but *spontaneous*. It is as if the signs emerge without the speaker's knowledge, in such a way that he is, as it were, hallucinated by the product of his own linguistic inventions. These associations of signifier and signified seem to form in spite of him, to the point that it is often he himself who is the most astonished.

This is a different kind of elaboration of linguistic signs from that of some delusional languages. In particular, there is no real dispersal or purely aleatory association between signifieds and signifiers, or between signifiers and signifieds. In this signifying crystallization, the signifiers are completely cut off from the phonemic oppositions usually codified in ordinary languages. The aleatory nature of such associations is nonetheless worth examining in the light of basic psychoanalytic principles.

These principles lead us to think that the invention of signifiers (which is the rule in glossolalia), like their relation with the signifieds, is only superficially random. In fact, what happens in glossolalia is primarily the result of a signifying capture, in that the structuring of the sign appears to be completely dependent on the unconscious primary process. This effect is so obvious in certain cases that the neologisms resulting from the subversive effects of condensation and displacement may be considered true signifying breakthroughs of the unconscious, in accordance with Lacan's theory of the unconscious structured like a language.

The Immutability of the Sign

We have just seen that the intrinsic arbitrariness of the sign is based on the fact that the signifier is freely chosen in relation to the idea it represents. But once it has been chosen, this signifier gains credence in the entire linguistic community, in the "speaking mass," to use Saussure's expression. This is how it becomes unchangeable. We have to admit, then, that the arbitrariness of the sign is in a way the cause of the subjection of a linguistic community to its language. As Saussure (1966) puts it: "No individual, even if he willed it, could modify in any way at all the choice that has been made; and what is more, the community itself cannot control so much as a single word; it is bound to the existing language" (p. 71).

The apparent fixity of language, which stems from the consensus adopted by the linguistic community, is therefore the source of the speaking subject's subjection to his language. By this arbitrary convention, the linguistic community necessarily establishes the sign in a tradition—or, to put it another way, in time. Yet there is the seed of an apparent contradiction here. As Saussure (1966) notes, there is

> a bond between the two antithetical forces—arbitrary convention by virtue of which choice is free, and time which causes choice to be fixed. Because the sign is arbitrary, it follows no law other than that of tradition, and because it is based on tradition, it is arbitrary. [p. 74]

But we must admit that, paradoxically, the temporal dimension is also what causes a certain alteration of the sign.

The Alteration of the Sign

Society's use of a language over a period of time modifies its signs. The sign may be durable because it is immutable, but it is also because it is temporally enduring that it can change. Here we are confronted with a relation of contradictory reciprocity between immutability and mutability. Changes in the sign involve both the signifier and the signified. On the level of the signifier, change is mostly on the phonetic level, but as for the signified, the change is in the concept as such. In other words, a change in the signified is coextensive with a modification in the understanding and the extension of the concept. In general, alteration of the sign comes under the heading of "a shift in the relationship between the signifier and the signified" (Saussure 1966, p. 74).

The Linear Nature of the Signifier

If changes in the sign are directly linked to the practice of a language over the course of time, the influence of the temporal factor is in turn inherently dependent on the nature of the signifier. The signifier itself is a phonemic sequence that unfolds over time. Speech, articulation, is nothing other than the actualization of the temporal unfolding of the signifier. This temporal span of the signifier is the source of a fundamental property of language: language unfolds in a directional manner that is called the *axis of oppositions* or the *syntagmatic axis*. It is this directionality in the organization of signifiers that Lacan calls the *signifying chain*.

At the same time as we establish the order of the sequence of signifiers, we presuppose another fundamental property of linguistic structures. Language is structured because it is already grounded in a set of given elements: the signs. But if all we had at our disposal were linguistic signs, we would not have a structural system—we would have only a lexicon. Language is a structure because, along with signs, it presupposes laws that govern them. These laws come into play in the context of the linearity of the signifier, with regard to two specific problems that are posed by the signifying chain: the problem of signifying concatenations and the question of substitutes that can take the place of existing elements. Every language has internal laws that differ according to whether they regulate concatenation or substitution. Language can therefore be analyzed from the point of view of two dimensions, each of which has its own specific properties: the *syntagmatic dimension* and the *paradigmatic dimension.*

THE TWO AXES OF LANGUAGE

After the definition of the linguistic sign, Saussure's (1966) second fundamental innovation was to distinguish a double division of the system of language. Given Lacan's particular use of this innovation, however, it is more relevant to examine it in the context of the work of Roman Jakobson (1956). When we speak, we perform two series of operations simultaneously: we *select* a certain number of linguistic units from the lexicon, and we *combine* them. Language is thus divided in two ways, by selection and by combination. Selection, the choice of one term from among others, implies that there are terms that can be interchanged. As for combination, it calls for a certain type of connection of the linguistic units, starting with the configuration of a certain order in the units of signification. This order can be diagrammed as a progression in complexity:

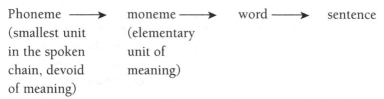

Phoneme ⟶ moneme ⟶ word ⟶ sentence
(smallest unit (elementary
in the spoken unit of
chain, devoid meaning)
of meaning)

The combination that involves the concatenation of linguistic units thus depends on a *relation of contiguity* among the signifying elements. More generally, there are two axes that divide the totality of language according to *selection* (the paradigmatic axis) and *combination* (the syntagmatic axis). Here we can identify Saussure's distinction between language [*langue*] and speech [*parole*]. Insofar as both of these are aspects of *langage*, each operates according to one or the other of the two axes. The axis of selection concerns the system of language [*langue*] in that it entails lexical choice, while speech [*parole*], the use of the chosen lexical terms, depends on the axis of combination. This is one of the reasons why Jakobson views a system of language according to whether its terms are associated by similarity or by contiguity. It is, in fact, his studies on aphasia (1956, 1964) that led to this conclusion.

Jakobson notes two major types of aphasia that are distinguished according to whether the selection process or the combination process is impaired. When the impairment affects lexical choice (selection), the aphasic has difficulty finding words. In place of the word he is seeking, he will often use a word that is in a *relation of contiguity* to it. Conversely, when it is the connecting of lexical terms (combination) that is impaired, the aphasic proceeds by *similarity*. These two pathological syndromes underscore a specific property of discourse: discourse unfolds according to two types of operations, *metaphoric* (on the axis of selection), and *metonymic* (on the axis of combination):

> The development of a discourse may take place along two different semantic lines: one topic may lead to another either through their similarity or through their contiguity. The *metaphoric way* would be the most appropriate term for the first case, and the *metonymic way* for the second, since they find their most condensed expression in metaphor and metonymy respectively. [Jakobson 1956, p. 77]

The following diagram sums up this division of language:

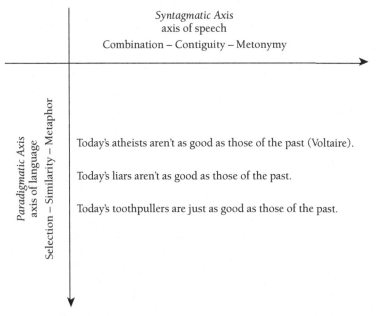

Syntagmatic Axis
axis of speech
Combination – Contiguity – Metonymy

Paradigmatic Axis
axis of language

Selection – Similarity – Metaphor

Today's atheists aren't as good as those of the past (Voltaire).

Today's liars aren't as good as those of the past.

Today's toothpullers are just as good as those of the past.

Consideration of the linguistic sign and of the division of language according to two axes leads us to the examination of two properties of language that will introduce us directly to fundamental points of Lacanian theory: *the value of the sign* and *metaphoric and metonymic constructions*. Saussure's definition of the value of the sign provides an approach to the Lacanian notion of the anchoring point [*point de capiton*].* Metaphor and metonymy lead to the fundamental Lacanian idea of the *primacy of the signifier* and to the consequences of this idea with regard to the *formations of the unconscious*.

---

*Translator's note: The *point de capiton* is, literally, a quilting point or point where an upholstery button is fastened.

5

The Value of the Linguistic Sign and Lacan's Anchoring Point

If "the linguistic entity exists only through the associating of the signifier and the signified" (Saussure 1966, p. 102), it is by definition *delimited*. This problem of the delimitation of the sign raises a number of issues, among them the critical question of the utterance, which for Lacan becomes so central to psychoanalysis that, as we shall see, he equates "the subject of the unconscious" and "the subject of desire" with "the subject of the utterance." Following Saussure, we may envisage the chain of speech as being double: a chain of concepts and a chain of acoustic images, such that any delimitation introduced into the chain of acoustic images entails a subsequent delimitation in the chain of concepts. This is illustrated by the following Saussurian schema (Saussure 1966, p. 104):

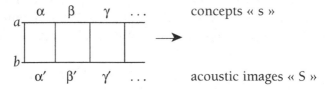

From this perspective, we may consider that the delimitation of *signifying elements* is always possible when they are taken in isolation. We have only to accept the principle of a one-to-one correspondence ($\alpha \rightarrow \alpha'$; $\beta \rightarrow \beta'$; $\gamma \rightarrow \gamma'$; . . .) between signifiers and signifieds to confirm the idea of such a delimitation. Moreover, the very notion of the linguistic sign leads to this idea. Since we know that there is a certain fixity in the relation between signifier and signified, we can imagine that each time we encounter a signifier S1 in the spoken chain, it is necessarily linked to a signified s1, which ensures a signification Sign. 1. This would imply that the signification is completely guaranteed when a linguistic sign is isolated from the chain. But such is by no means the case, since a given acoustic image does not allow for a given signification when the sign is isolated from other signs. Let's take a look at an example from Saussure. A single spoken acoustic image may be linked to two possible signifieds, producing two different significations:

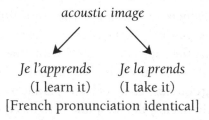

acoustic image

Je l'apprends   *Je la prends*
(I learn it)   (I take it)
[French pronunciation identical]

This acoustic image may therefore be derived from two distinctly different signs; only the context of the spoken chain allows us to define its signification. The delimitation of the sign is thus coextensive with the delimitation of the signification. Hence Saussure (1966) recommends this rule for delimiting the sign:

> [To] be assured that we are really dealing with a unit, we
> must be able in comparing a series of sentences in which the
> same unit occurs to separate the unit from the rest of the
> context and find in each instance that the meaning justifies
> the delimitation. [pp. 104–105]

To say that it is the context that delimits the sign means
simply that the sign is a sign only as a function of its context.
Since this context is a set of other signs, the reality of the linguistic sign exists only as a function of all these other signs. It is
this property that Saussure calls the *value of the sign*. The value
is what makes an acoustic fragment become real and concrete,
what delimits it as making sense, and, therefore, what makes it
a linguistic sign. As Saussure points out, "each linguistic term
derives its value from its opposition to all the other terms" in
the same way as, in chess, "the respective value of the pieces
depends on their position on the chessboard" (p. 88). In language as in chess, the value of the terms depends on an established set of rules.

The notion of *value* provides us with one of the most telling justifications for seeing language as a *structural system*. Linguistic signs are meaningful not only because of their content,
but also—indeed primarily—because of the oppositional relations between them within the spoken chain. Therefore, in the
final analysis, it is the system that gives them their signifying
identities. Language is a series of divisions simultaneously
introduced into a flux of thoughts and a flux of sounds. Since
"language works out its units while taking shape between two
shapeless masses" (p. 112), the linguistic sign corresponds to a
connection of these two amorphous masses: an idea is fixed in a
sound at the same time as a phonic sequence constitutes itself
as the signifier of an idea. Hence Saussure's famous metaphor:

> Language can . . . be compared to a sheet of paper: thought
> is the front and the sound the back; one cannot cut the front
> without cutting the back at the same time; likewise in lan-
> guage, one can neither divide sound from thought nor
> thought from sound. [p. 113]

In conclusion, then, we can see that language is first and foremost a system of differences and oppositions between elements. It is as if the structure of the linguistic sign were the result of a "cut" occurring in the flux of sound and thoughts. "Whether we take the signified or the signifier, language has neither ideas nor sounds that existed before the linguistic system, but only conceptual and phonic differences that have issued from the system" (Saussure 1966, p. 120).

If the signifier comes into being through such a cut, there is no "flux of signifiers" properly speaking. It is the occurrence of the cut that creates the order of the signifier at the same time as it associates the signifier to a concept. The emergence of the signifier is therefore inseparable from the creation of the linguistic sign in its totality.

Lacan modifies Saussure's theses in certain ways. (See Nancy and Lacoue-Labarthe 1992.) The flux of thoughts and the flux of sounds are, without further ado, termed the flux of signifieds and the flux of signifiers. And, as Lacan writes it, the schema of the linguistic sign is inverted:

$$\frac{S}{s}$$

The problem is thus reformulated by Lacan as the mode of relation of a flux of signifiers to a flux of signifieds. This relation also undergoes an important change with respect to Saussure. Lacan does not subscribe to the notion of a "cut" that unites the signifier and the signified and at the same time determines them both. Instead, he presents this delimitation through an original concept that he calls the anchoring point.

This innovation is directly based on psychoanalytic experience, which shows us that the relation of the signifier to the signified "always appears fluid, always ready to come undone" (Lacan 1955–1956, p. 261). The Lacanian concept of delimitation by the anchoring point is reinforced by the very foundation of psychotic experience, in which it is precisely this type of knotting that seems to be absent.

A preliminary remark concerning the anchoring point is necessary. This concept has the value of "delimitation" in the Saussurian sense, but it takes on its full meaning in Lacan's thought only when it is brought into relation with the register of desire. In fact, the anchoring point is the basic constituent of the Graph of Desire that Lacan developed in the course of two successive seminars, "The Formations of the Unconscious" (Lacan 1957–1958) and "Desire and its Interpretation" (Lacan 1958–1959). The theoretical elaborations that he sets forth in these two unpublished seminars may be found in condensed form in his essay "The Subversion of the subject and the dialectic of desire in the Freudian unconscious" (Lacan 1960b). But in 1956 Lacan (1955–1956) had already proposed the notion of the anchoring point, with the clear intention of questioning the limitations of the Saussurian correspondence between the flux of signifiers and the flux of signifieds and of replacing it with a more adequate explanation based on analytic experience. ("A step forward has to be taken in order to give what is involved here a sense that is really usable in our experience. Saussure tries to define a correspondence between these two flows that would segment them. But the sole fact that his solution is inconclusive, since it leaves the locution and the whole sentence problematic, clearly shows both the sense and the limitations of his method" [Lacan 1955–1956, p. 262].)

For Lacan, the anchoring point is above all the operation by which "the signifier stops the otherwise determinate sliding of signification" (Lacan 1960b, p. 303). In other words, it is because of this that the signifier is associated with the signified in the chain of discourse. The anchoring point is represented graphically in this way:

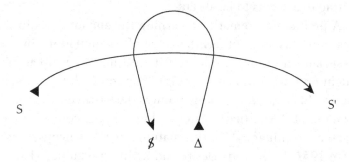

In this diagram, the vector $\overrightarrow{\Delta \$}$ represents the anchoring point, "hooking" the signifying chain SS' at two points. Here there is a certain analogy with Saussure's "cut," where a series of simultaneous caesurae, $\frac{\alpha}{\alpha'}; \frac{\beta}{\beta'}; \frac{\gamma}{\gamma'}$, determines the units of signification. But for Lacan the delimitation of signification is, from the start, restricted to the set of the spoken sequence and not to successive elementary units.

> The diachronic function of this anchoring point is to be found in the sentence, in that the sentence completes its signification only with its last term, each term being anticipated in the construction of [all] the others, and, inversely, sealing their meaning by its retroactive effect. [Lacan 1960b, p. 303; translation modified]

This is a direct reference to the problem of the value of the sign analyzed by Saussure. A sign is meaningful only in the relation of opposition that it maintains with all the other signs in the spoken sequence. One might therefore propose, as does Lacan, that a sign can make sense only retroactively, since the signification of a message emerges only at the end of the signifying utterance itself. This retroactive dimension of meaning is represented in the diagram of the anchoring point by the reverse direction of the vector $\overrightarrow{\Delta \beta}$; in other words it is *after the fact* that the anchoring point stops the sliding of signification. The ambiguity of the problem of the utterance depends, to a great extent, on this delimitation of meaning "after the fact" of articulation.

Further study of the way the signifying utterance unfolds in the spoken sequence involves an examination of its consequences on the two semantic levels of metaphor and metonymy, which underlie the process of language in the paradigmatic and syntagmatic directions.

6

Metaphor, Metonymy, and the Primacy of the Signifier

Given the notion of the anchoring point, another step may be taken in the introduction to the linguistic reference as the basis of Lacan's psychoanalytic elaborations. This advance toward what will ultimately become the "logic of the signifier" starts with an analysis of the metaphoric and metonymic processes in the subject's discourse as irrefutable evidence of the primordial character of the signifier.

A few chronological reference points will help us follow Lacan's approach to the comparison of unconscious mechanisms with those of language. Lacan's first explicit references to metaphor and metonymy appear in his authoritative discussion of the Schreber case (Freud 1911) in the seminar *The Psychoses* (Lacan 1955–1956). We also find these notions developed in the seminar on *Object Relations* (Lacan 1956–1957; see especially the session of May 8, 1957).

In analyzing the case of President Schreber, Lacan (1955–1956) concludes that in delusion it is as though there were a progressive invasion of the signifier, in the sense that the signifier gradually breaks free of its signified. This conclusion is reinforced by the study of the mechanism of metaphor, which reveals the primordial nature of the signifier in relation to the signified. These two arguments allow Lacan to advance the thesis of the primacy of the signifier as best defining the only true return to Freud. He symbolizes the primacy of the signifier over the signified twice over: first, by inverting the Saussurian algorithm for the linguistic sign; second, by representing the signifier by a capital S:

$$\frac{S}{s}$$

The position of the letter S above the bar indicates the primacy of the signifier. Lacan concludes from analytic experience that the signifier not only governs the subject's discourse, it governs the subject himself. Proof of this is the crucial role played by the metaphoric and metonymic functions in the advent of unconscious processes and, more generally, in neurotic and psychotic phenomena, a role that was already central in the original Freudian discovery.

> As a rule, we always give precedence to the signified in our analyses, because it's certainly what is most seductive and what seems at first to be the dimension appropriate to symbolic investigation in psychoanalysis. But in misrecognizing the primary mediating role of the signifier, in misrecognizing that it is the signifier that in reality is the guiding element, not only do we throw the original understanding of neurotic phenomena, the interpretation of dreams itself, out of balance, but we make ourselves absolutely incapable of understanding what is happening in the psychoses. . . .
>
>   The opposition between metaphor and metonymy is fundamental, since what Freud originally emphasized in the mechanisms of neurosis, as well as in those of the marginal

phenomena of normal life or of dreams, is neither the metaphoric dimension nor identification. It's the opposite. In
general, what Freud calls condensation is what in rhetoric
we call metaphor. What he calls displacement is metonymy.
The structuration, the lexical existence of the entirety of the
signifying apparatus, determines the phenomena present in
neurosis, because the signifier is the instrument by which
the missing signified expresses itself. This is why, when we
turn our attention back to the signifier, we're doing nothing
other than returning to the starting point of the Freudian
discovery. [Lacan 1955–1956, pp. 220–221, translation
modified]

In these elements of Lacan's thought we find all the principal theoretical arguments justifying the thesis that the unconscious is structured like a language. The primacy of the signifier
is attested to by the metaphoric and metonymic mechanisms;
these mechanisms are assimilated to the functioning of the primary process (condensation and displacement); and, finally, they
are extended to the configuration of the formations of the unconscious. We must, therefore, address these fundamental points
in detail, starting with the problem of metaphor and the illustration of the primacy of the signifier that Lacan presents in the
seminar on "The Purloined Letter" (Lacan 1955).

THE METAPHORIC PROCESS

Metaphor is traditionally classed as a trope, a stylistic figure based
on relations of similarity, of substitution. In this sense it is a
linguistic mechanism that operates along the synchronic (or
paradigmatic) axis, that is, along the axis of the lexicon or of
language [la langue]. Moreover, it is a process of lexical enrich-

ment, if only because many "figurative meanings" were originally metaphors.

In principle, metaphor consists in referring to something
by the name of something else. It is, then, in the full sense of
the term what Lacan calls *signifying substitution*. Insofar as metaphor shows how the signifieds obtain their coherence only from
the network of signifiers, the nature of this signifying substitution demonstrates the *autonomy of the signifier in relation to the
signified*, and, consequently, the *primacy of the signifier*.

Let us look at an appropriate example: the metaphorical use
of the term "plague" to designate psychoanalysis:

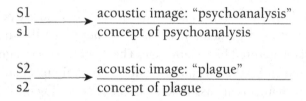

$$\frac{S1}{s1} \longrightarrow \frac{\text{acoustic image: "psychoanalysis"}}{\text{concept of psychoanalysis}}$$

$$\frac{S2}{s2} \longrightarrow \frac{\text{acoustic image: "plague"}}{\text{concept of plague}}$$

When we introduce the metaphoric figure, we perform a signifying substitution which consists, here, in substituting S2 for S1.

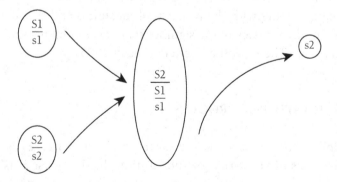

The substitution of S2 for S1 puts $\frac{S1}{s1}$ under the bar of signification. So it is as if the sign $\frac{S1}{s1}$ has become the new signifier

for S2. In fact, it is the signification resulting from the original association of S1 and s1 that serves as signified at the end of the metaphorical operation. On the other hand, the signified s2 (the idea of sickness) has been expelled, and we have to perform a mental operation in order to retrieve it.

A comment is necessary here to bring us back to the aleatory nature of the sign. In metaphor, the signified associated with the substitutive signifier (S2) is inevitably a sign, $\frac{S1}{s1}$. In fact, if the process of signifying substitution consisted simply in a permutation of the signifier, we would have a new sign and not a metaphor. We would end up with $\frac{S2}{s2}$, which would be a new lexical term. We would thus be back with the situation mentioned earlier, in which one and the same signifier (S2) can be associated with any signified (s2, then s1). What we are dealing with here, then, is an aleatory association between signifier and signified.

In the network of signifiers in the spoken sequence where metaphor operates, it is therefore $\frac{S1}{s1}$ that is immediately associated with S2 as its signified. This reveals a specific property of language, namely that the chain of signifiers governs the set of signifieds. Conversely, the signifieds derive their coherence entirely from the network of signifiers. Under these conditions, language [*langue*] governs speech [*parole*], which constitutes the manifest proof of the *primacy of the signifier*.

Lacan's masterful account of Poe's story "The Purloined Letter" (Lacan 1954–1955, 1955) exemplifies this principle. We may recall that Poe's story presents a series of characters who are stirred up about a letter whose circulation is the main attraction of the story.

In the first scene the Queen, who has just received a letter, hurries to hide it before the arrival of the King and his Minister, fearing that they may find there information that might compromise her honor. The concealment of the letter does not escape the attention of the shrewd Minister, who suspects what might be going on when he notes the Queen's discomposure. He takes an apparently similar letter out of his coat, pretends to read it openly, and exchanges it for the Queen's letter, which he then takes. The Queen has observed this substitution with alarm, but she dares not say anything since she must keep the King off the track. At the end of this first episode the Queen knows that the Minister has gotten possession of the letter, and the Minister knows that the Queen knows this.

In the course of the second episode, a new character, Dupin, makes his entrance. Under orders from the Police Commissioner, Dupin pays a visit to the Minister, expecting that he will find the letter. The Minister, suspecting the motive for Dupin's visit, receives him as if nothing were out of the ordinary. During his inspection, Dupin notices a crumpled paper, casually placed in full view. He understands that this is surely the letter he has been looking for, consigned to the very best of hiding places. He deliberately "forgets" his snuffbox at the Minister's home, and takes his leave. Under the pretext of retrieving his forgotten property, Dupin goes back to see the Minister the following day, bringing with him a perfect facsimile of the crumpled document. He takes advantage of an incident that diverts the Minister's attention to substitute the fake letter for the coveted one and then leaves.

The second scene thus represents a strategy of exchange that inverts that of the preceding episode: it is now Dupin who has the letter, and the Minister the counterfeit. However, the Minister is unaware of the substitution, whereas the Queen knows what happened.

The Lacanian interpretation of Poe's story is a model of clarity. If we consider that the letter is invested with the function of the signifier, and its contents with that of the signified, we can see how the signifier has primacy over the subject. As the plot unfolds, each character is taken in by the play of the successive substitutions of the circulating letter. The King is fooled insofar as he sees nothing of what is going on. The Queen, for her part, sees everything but is powerless to act. Finally, the Minister neither sees nor finds out about Dupin's substitution.

Each character in turn is stirred to action by the circulation of the letter. Given the very unusual nature of this motivation, Lacan can show in detail how the power of the signifier is capable of mobilizing the subject. The letter does duty as a signifier, since it affects characters who are unaware of its contents (the signified). In addition, we note that this unique signifier continues its course in spite of the muteness of some characters and the blindness of others. We can find no better metaphoric illustration of the order of the unconscious and the process by which it emerges; it is something that is always there, but also and at the same time always elsewhere. The vicissitudes of the letter/signifier, which is replaced by several substitutes along the way, inevitably call to mind the order of language and its mechanisms of signifying substitution. One final analogy: the actions of each of the characters are determined in relation to the letter in the same way that the subject, without being aware of it, is acted upon by the signifiers of language in relation to the unconscious.

The primacy of the signifier thus entails the *domination of the subject by the signifier*, which predetermines him precisely at the point where he believes he can escape determination by a language he ostensibly controls. This essential property seals the relation of the subject to his discourse and is at the very foundation of Lacan's notion of the "speakingbeing" [*le parlêtre*].

This analysis of the metaphoric process has led to the following basic conclusions:

1. The metaphoric process generates meaning insofar as it is supported by the autonomy of the signifier in relation to the signified. This explains Lacan's formula: "metaphor occurs at the precise point at which sense emerges from non-sense" (Lacan 1957a, p. 158).
2. The principle of the construction of metaphor attests to the primacy of the signifier, in that it is the chain of signifiers that governs the network of signifieds.
3. The primacy of the signifier operates not only with regard to the signified but also with regard to the subject, who, unwittingly, is predetermined by it.

These three points will be amply confirmed by the analysis of the metonymic process, which will bring us to the same conclusions.

THE METONYMIC PROCESS

Etymologically, the term *metonymy* means change of name (*metonomia*). This stylistic figure works according to a process of transfer of denomination by means of which an object is designated by a term other than the one that usually belongs to it. This transfer of denomination from one term to another, however, is possible only under certain conditions of linkage between the two terms.

These conditions are traditionally specified according to the following modes. The two terms may be linked by a relation of material to object or of container to contents, for example, "a brass band" or "to drink a cup." The relation may also be one of part to whole: "a sail on the horizon" or "drive a six-cylinder," or of cause for effect, for example, "harvest" (which designates not only the activity of harvesting but also the effect of that activity). Let us examine the construction of a fashionable metonymic expression: "to be on the couch," meaning "to be in analysis." Here the term "couch" is metonymically assigned to replace the term "analysis." In other words, the part (couch) is used for the whole (analysis). Even if the whole is not mentioned, the meaning comes through because of the relation of contiguity between part and whole.

The metonymic process, then, establishes a new signifier that is in a relation of contiguity to a prior signifier that it replaces. We can diagram the process by means of the following algorithm:

$$\frac{S1}{s1} \longrightarrow \frac{\text{the acoustic image: "analysis"}}{\text{the idea of being in analysis}}$$

$$\frac{S2}{s2} \longrightarrow \frac{\text{the acoustic image: "couch"}}{\text{the idea of a couch}}$$

Introducing the metonymy brings about a signifying substitution in which S2 is substituted for S1:

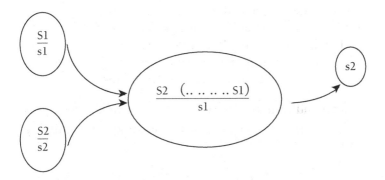

But, as opposed to what happens in metaphor, the "expelled" signifier does not go under the bar of signification. It remains above the bar, since, in metonymy, meaning is dependent on the retention of S1 in immediate contiguity with S2 and in association with s1. On the other hand, s2 is provisionally expelled. Here we can make the same remark as in the case of metaphor: in the metonymic construction, the retention of the two signifiers guarantees against any possibility of devising a new sign that would arbitrarily associate a signifier with a signified.

For reasons similar to those given in the study of metaphor, metonymy also demonstrates the autonomy of signifiers with regard to the network of signifieds that they govern, and consequently the primacy of the signifier. Lacan uses algorithms to represent these properties of the signifier in the metaphorical and metonymic processes. The metaphoric process is first symbolized as follows:

$$ f\left(\frac{S'}{S}\right) S \cong S\ (+)s $$

Lacan explains that

> it is in the substitution of signifier for signifier that an effect of signification is produced that is creative or poetic, in other words, which is the advent of the signification in question. . . . The sign + between ( ) represents here the crossing of the bar — and the constitutive value of this crossing for the emergence of signification. [Lacan 1957a, p. 164]

In a second formula devised at the same time, Lacan puts a stronger accent on the nature of metaphor as signifying substitution:

$$ \frac{S}{\not{S}'} \cdot \frac{\not{S}'}{x} \rightarrow S\left(\frac{U}{s}\right) $$

He explains that in this new diagram

the capital Ss are signifiers, x the unknown signification and s the signified induced by the metaphor, which consists of the substitution in the signifying chain of S for S'. The elision of S', represented here by the bar through it, is the condition of the success of the metaphor. [Lacan 1955–1956, p. 200][1]

This alternative formulation has the advantage of constituting a general matrix for metaphor that is directly applicable to the inaugural metaphorical process known as the *metaphor of the Name-of-the-Father*, or *paternal metaphor*. Although we will examine the meaning of this metaphor later on, we present its formula here (Lacan 1955–1956, p. 200)[2]:

$$\frac{\text{Name-of-the-Father}}{\text{Desire of the Mother}} \cdot \frac{\text{Desire of the Mother}}{\text{Signified to the subject}} \longrightarrow \text{Name-of-the-Father}\left(\frac{O}{\text{Phallus}}\right)$$

The formulation of the *metonymic process* calls for the same symbols in an expression whose function is to connect a new signifier to an old one with which it is in a relation of contiguity, the new one replacing the original:

$$f\ (S \ldots\ldots S')\ S \cong S\ (-)\ s$$

Lacan draws our attention to this difference between metonymy and metaphor:

The sign – placed between ( ) represents here the maintenance of the bar — which, in the original algorithm, marks the irreducibility in which, in the relations of the signifier to the signified, the resistance to signification is constituted. [Lacan 1957a, p. 164, translation modified][3]

---

1. Translator's note: "U" represents "Unconscious."
2. Translator's note: "O" stands for "Other," to be explained further on.
3. The original algorithm is $\frac{S}{s}$.

The function of maintaining the bar in metonymy is in fact proof of a resistance to signification, since this stylistic figure always presents itself as apparent non-sense (one is not simply *on a couch*, one is analyzed on a couch). In other words, a mental operation is always necessary to grasp the meaning of the metonymic expression by re-establishing the connection between S and S'. In metaphor, on the other hand, if the emergence of meaning is immediate this is precisely because the bar has been crossed.

In the Lacanian perspective, the notions of metaphor and metonymy constitute two of the cornerstones of the structural conception of the unconscious process. They support a large part of the theoretical edifice founded on the thesis that the unconscious is structured like a language. In addition, if the metaphoric and metonymic processes are at the very source of the mechanisms that generally regulate the functioning of the unconscious, we should be able to show how these two paradigms can be applied both on the level of the primary process and on the level of the formations of the unconscious strictly speaking. We propose to illustrate just such an application in the context of our examination of the following themes:

—the process of *condensation* in dreams as a metaphoric process
—the process of *displacement* in dreams as a metonymic mechanism
—*neologisms, glossolalia,* and *delusional languages* as metaphoric and metonymic constructions
—the *symptom* as metaphor
—the *joke* as a metaphoric condensation and/or a metonymic displacement

—the *process of desire* as a metonymic development
—the metaphor of the Name-of-the-Father, or paternal metaphor, as a *means of access to the symbolic order.*

The whole of the theoretical work set forth in *The Interpretation of Dreams* (Freud 1900) leads us to assume that, although he could not explain them, Freud intuitively knew about the two principal axes of language, substitution/metaphor and combination/metonymy. It is these intuitions ascribed to Freud that Lacan develops, chiefly in the direction of a rapprochement between the linguistic data and the primary-process mechanisms of condensation and displacement. We have seen that the idea of such a rapprochement antecedes Lacan's theoretical reflection (see Freeman Sharpe 1937). Nonetheless, Lacan codifies it in an apposite and vigorous theoretical procedure that follows Freud's text to the letter.

7

Condensation as a Metaphoric Process

To return to the process of condensation as Freud (1900) discusses it in "The Interpretation of Dreams": we have seen that Freud distinguishes several forms of condensation. Let us take a closer look at one of these, condensation by omission. The "dream of the botanical monograph" is a remarkable example of this mechanism of condensation. Indeed, the manifest content here appears to be radically overdetermined, since most of its elements relate back to a multiplicity of latent elements via associative chains. This is particularly true for the terms "botanical" and "monograph." ("This first investigation leads us to conclude that the elements 'botanical' and 'monograph' found their way into the content of the dream because they possessed copious contacts with the majority of the dream-thoughts, because, that is to say, they constituted 'nodal points' upon which a great number of the dream-thoughts converged, and because they had several meanings in connection with the interpretation of the dream" [Freud 1900, p. 283].) But what do these terms have to do with the metaphoric process?

We recall that, according to Lacan, metaphor is a *signifying substitution* because it involves the substitution of one signifier for another. In language [*langage*], this substitution most often takes place between two terms thanks to a semantic or a homophonic similarity. It is clear that this similarity is not always immediately identifiable when it occurs on an unconscious level. Only the associative chains can reveal it.

In the "dream of the botanical monograph," the term *monograph* ($\frac{S3}{s3}$) substitutes for latent terms such as "the one-sidedness of my studies" ($\frac{S1}{s1}$) and "the costliness of my favorite hobbies" $\frac{S2}{s2}$.

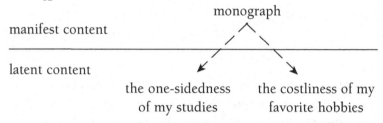

We thus find, after a fashion, the metaphoric process at work as described in Chapter 6 above:

Let $\frac{S3}{s3}$ = botanical monograph

$\frac{S1}{s1}$ = the one-sidedness of my studies

$\frac{S2}{s2}$ = the costliness of my favorite hobbies

The metaphoric process functions in the dream in the following way:

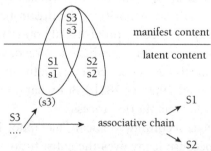

This construction illustrates an application of the metaphoric mechanism described by the formula:

In other words, condensation may be considered to be strictly analogous to a signifying substitution. The analysis of the functioning of the term *botanical* would lead to the same conclusion.

The type of condensation that Freud calls *composite structure* also reveals the workings of a metaphoric mechanism. In this case the latent elements that present shared characteristics fuse together, so that they are all represented on the manifest level by a single element. This is how the composite characters, collective figures, and neological composites that inhabit our dreams are made.[1]

In the "dream of Irma's injection" (Freud 1900), Freud discovers that Irma appears in a series of situations in which each of her actions refers back to different people.

> None of these figures whom I lighted upon by following up
> "Irma" appeared in the dream in bodily shape. They were

---

1. "The process of condensation further explains certain constituents of the content of dreams which are peculiar to them and not found in waking ideation. What I have in mind are 'collective' and 'composite figures' and the strange 'composite structures', which are creations not unlike the composite animals invented by the folk-imagination of the Orient. . . . There are many sorts of ways in which figures of this kind can be put together. I may build up a figure by giving it the features of two people; or I may give it the *form* of one person but think of it in the dream as having the *name* of another person; or I may have a visual picture of one person, but put it in a situation which is appropriate to another" (Freud 1901a, pp. 650–651).

concealed behind the dream figure of "Irma," which was thus turned into a collective image with, it must be admitted, a number of contradictory characteristics. Irma became the representative of all these other figures which had been sacrificed to the work of condensation, since I passed over to *her*, point by point, everything that reminded me of *them*. [p. 293]

Another example of condensation in the same dream aptly illustrates the metaphoric process. "Doctor M." is a metaphoric elaboration of two latent elements: the actual person M. and Freud's eldest brother.[2] They have certain traits in common, which is why they lend themselves so well to metaphoric substitution:

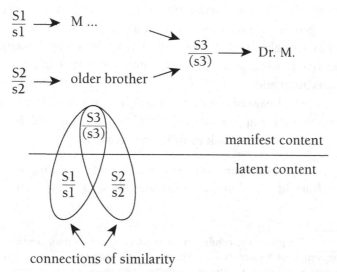

connections of similarity

_____

2. "There is another way in which a 'collective figure' can be produced for purposes of dream-condensation, namely, by uniting the actual features of two or more people into a single dream-image. It was in this way that the Dr. M. of my dream was constructed. He bore the name of Dr. M., he spoke and acted like him; but his physical characteristics and his malady belonged

The neological composition of the term *propyls* provides another example of this process in the "Dream of Irma's Injection." *Propyls* is the product of a signifying substitution that has two latent elements, "Propylaea" and "amyls," that have certain similar properties.[3]

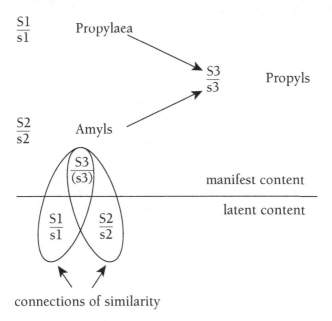

connections of similarity

to someone else, namely to my eldest brother. One single feature, his pale appearance, was doubly determined, since it was common to both of them in real life" (Freud 1990, p. 293).

3. Freud (1900) gives an example of the same type with another neologism produced in a dream: "Norekdal." This term is a condensation of "Nora" and "Ekdal" (Cf. 1900, p. 296). The same metaphorical mechanism often appears in a stereotyped manner in psychopathological alterations of language like glossolalia and certain delusional languages. In these cases the neological productions are often accompanied by metonymic mechanisms, as I have shown in an earlier study (Dor 1982).

These few examples are so telling that further illustrations would be superfluous. They are sufficient to attest to the fact that in dream work the processes of condensation are analogous to the metaphoric processes of language. An analogy of the same type may be made between the mechanism of displacement and the metonymic process.

8

Displacement and Dream Work as Metonymic Processes

Latent elements are not always condensed during dream work, since the greater part of this material may at times be represented on the manifest level. Nonetheless, with the exception of children's dreams, these latent elements are not represented as they are. There is a reversal of values on the level of the manifest representation. Strictly speaking, we have here a displacement of values that brings about a displacement of meaning (see Chapter 2).[1]

In irrational dreams this displacement of value is most often total, and the essential part of the latent material becomes perfectly secondary at the manifest level. In such cases this mechanism allows us to identify the configuration of the metonymic process. The representation of the essential by the incidental is, in a way, the representation of the whole by a part. It is also

---

1. "We may put it this way: *in the course of the dream work the psychical intensity passes over from the thoughts and ideas to which it properly belongs on to others which in our judgment have no claim to any such emphasis*" (Freud 1901a, p. 654).

analogous to other major instances of metonymy (the representation of the content by the container, of the cause by the effect), in which one signifier expresses another with which it is in a relation of contiguity (see Chapter 6).

If, in the dream, the manifest nonessential element expresses the latent primary element through a metonymic construction, it remains the case that the relation of contiguity between the signifiers is never so directly obvious as in the metonymic elaborations of language. This relation of contiguity can be revealed only by associations.

Let us examine this process with a sample dream reported by Angel Garma:[2]

> I'm walking in the streets of Sofia with my governess. I go down streets where there are brothels. I'm French, and I'm there as a French person. I see a friend who has recently had a skiing accident. I tell him I'm French and joyfully show him my French identity card. [Garma 1954, p. 24]

Analysis of the elements "I am French" and "skiing accident" shows that they have undergone a significant displacement of value, that is, of meaning, in the dream. The associative work allows us to decode the latent signification that is disguised by metonymy on the manifest level. Garma's account of the associations is as follows:

"It could be seen that the elements which stand out as the principal components of the manifest content of the dream are far from playing the same part in the dream-thoughts. And, as a corollary, the converse of this assertion can be affirmed: what is clearly the essence of the dream-thoughts need not be represented in the dream at all. The dream is, as it were, differently centered from the dream-thoughts—its content has different elements as its central point" (Freud 1900, p. 305).

2. Translator's note: The English-language edition [Garma 1966] was unavailable to me; I am translating here from the French edition.

Sometimes he thinks he does not deserve to be French, because he is not brave enough. The history of France is a history of courageous actions. In his country of origin, where
there still exist harsh customs of Arab influence, France has
the reputation of being the country of love. According to the
patient's associations, being French means being courageous
in love, that is, having genital relations and overcoming all
the fears that make him impotent. . . .

    The friend in question in *I see a friend* is someone who
has intimate relations with many women. The *skiing accident* is an accident this friend really had a while before. But
this brings to the patient's mind another accident, the gonorrhea contracted recently by this friend's brother. The skiing accident in the dream's manifest content is a typical displacement and represents the latent idea of possible accidents
due to sexual relations. [Garma 1954, p. 24]

This example, then, reveals a double displacement: "I am
French" means having normal sexual relations with women;
"skiing accident" represents ideas of possible accidental consequences of sexual relations and, more generally, the dangers of
sexuality. In other words, the displacement imposes manifest
material to designate contiguous latent materials. In this dream
there is, therefore, a transfer of denomination identical with the
mechanism of metonymy that always imposes a new signifier in
a relation of contiguity with the prior signifier it replaces.

    In accordance with the diagram illustrating the mechanism
of metonymy (see Chapter 6), we can represent this transfer of
denomination in the following way:

$$\frac{S2}{s2} \left\{ \begin{array}{l} \text{"I am French"} \\ \text{"skiing accident"} \end{array} \right.$$

$$\frac{S1}{s1} \left\{ \begin{array}{l} \text{"having normal sexual relations with women"} \\ \text{"the risk of sexual accidents"} \end{array} \right.$$

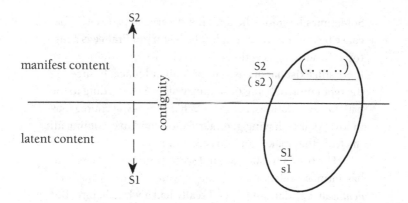

The manifest material $\frac{S2}{s2}$ ("skiing accident") does not immediately make sense on account of the presence of the signified (s2) associated with it. Because it will be eliminated by the metonymic construction, this signified is put in parentheses. The contiguity that makes the metonymic construction possible appears in the associative chain. The element $\frac{S1}{s1}$ ("sexual accidents") is metonymically linked to element $\frac{S2}{s2}$ ("skiing accident") by virtue of an associative link: his friend's brother accidentally contracted gonorrhea.

Displacement operates in the dream according to a process whose metonymic outcome may be illustrated as follows:

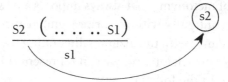

On a larger scale, the overall process of dream work is a metonymic enterprise. As such, it is, as it were, based on a general mechanism of transfer of denomination that Freud calls the disguising or distortion of meaning. A dream offers resistance to signification precisely because this resistance is the product of the dream work. Here Lacan provides a telling detail when he observes that the resistance to signification of a metonymy is due to the fact that metonymy always appears to be nonsensical.

Examination of another dream immediately confirms this metonymic function of the dream work as a whole.

> "In a room with my husband. I have a lot of trouble finding the gas valve. When I open it, the gas comes out. Little by little the house tumbles down. We are going to die. At the same time, I see the house rising up again." [Garma 1954, p. 267]

The analysis of the dream gradually reveals the following meaning:

> It is the dream of a woman whose husband is impotent, and who wants a divorce. The room represents living together with the husband. The penis is represented by the gas valve and impotence by the difficulties in finding it. The destruction of the house and approaching death are the end of the marriage. The house rising up again represents a new marriage. [Garma 1954, p. 267]

We cannot say that, strictly speaking, the "difficulty in finding the gas valve" signifies "the husband's impotence." This seems like nonsense. The resistance to signification depends at least partially on the chain of various intermediary materials placed in connection by the dream work itself. Thus, if the analysis of the dream is a dismantling of the dream work through the traversing of the chain of contiguous elements, when all is said and done what we are dealing with is a metonymic progression.

9

The Joke as a
Metaphoric–Metonymic Process

The structural analogy between certain processes of language and certain unconscious processes that we have seen in dreams also exists in other formations of the unconscious, if not in all of them. The joke is an interesting example of an unconscious formation that combines both metaphoric condensation and metonymic displacement.

Quite early on, Freud detected the structural identity underlying the mechanism of condensation and the construction of certain jokes.

> I have described as a part of this dream-work a process of condensation which shows the greatest similarity to the one found in the technique of jokes—which, like it, leads to abbreviation, and creates substitute-formations of the same character. [Freud 1905b, p. 28]

In fact, the joke can put together condensations like those we saw in the "propyls" and "Norekdal" examples. In other words, the joke, too, works through signifying substitution, through metaphor. Freud (1905b) demonstrates this in the first chapter of his book on jokes with his analysis of Heinrich Heine's well-known witticism *famillionaire*. (This condensation will be discussed in detail in Chapter 23 below.) Here is how the metaphoric condensation is constructed:

FAMILI   AR
MILLIONAIRE
FAMILLIONAIRE

Freud (1905b) likewise explains a similar construction, *Carthaginoiserie*, coined by Sainte-Beuve in his discussion of Flaubert's novel *Salammbô*, which is set in Carthage.

CARTHAGINOIS
CHINOISERIE
CARTHAGINOISERIE

The elaboration of a joke may be based on another technique that makes use of the unconscious register of displacement. According to Freud (1905b), this consists in "the diversion of the train of thought, the displacement of the psychical emphasis on to a topic other than the opening one" (p. 51). This technique therefore follows the path of *metonymy*. Let us take a closer look at the metonymic structure of the witticism in a clinical vignette where its special interest lies in its having been completely involuntary. In other words, we shall see that the joke, structured metonymically, substitutes for another formation of the unconscious, the slip of the tongue.

A young woman who had just returned from a honeymoon trip to North Africa announced to her analyst, in a splendid denial, that she had had "a very exciting *wedding veilage*." Her own words left her stupefied for a moment, but it soon became evident, in the course of the session, that her husband had not really been equal to the occasion during the trip, and that it was becoming hard for her to keep on suppressing intense unconscious feelings of recrimination. Her reproach came out through a displacement that facilitated the witticism as well as the slip of the tongue. The meaning of this "mixed" formation of the unconscious was brought out in a series of associations that revealed the underlying metonymic construction.

For this woman, the honeymoon "voyage" was first and foremost associated with the wild enthusiasm of her passion and her impatiently looking forward to its satisfaction. On the other hand, the "veilage" referred to the veils worn by North African women that, *for the patient*, symbolized a degree of erotic servitude, of hardship in matters of love. Although the symbol of the veil also functioned as an unconscious signifier of the hymen, it was mainly the idea of this erotic misfortune that was immediately associated with her sexual disappointment.

The relation of contiguity between "wedding" and "veilage" was amply sufficient for the metonymy to function as a joke/slip of the tongue. In other words, there had been metonymic displacement, that is, a transfer of denomination. The mechanism can be described as follows:

The element "wedding voyage" ($\frac{S1}{s1}$) was above all the occasion of disappointment in love, of an erotic humiliation that the patient was trying hard to forget. The return of the repressed occurred by means of a signifying displacement brought about by an associative element, "erotic servitude," that provided the contiguity with the metonymic element "wedding veilage."

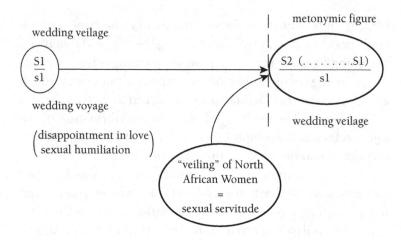

In conclusion, I may add that this woman's distressing experience during her "wedding voyage/veilage" was so unsettling that we were able to define it as the origin of a symptom that developed later and, as we shall see, took a spectacular metaphoric form.

10

The Symptom as a Metaphoric Process

Let us take another look at the clinical vignette of the patient's bitterness at her husband's impotence during their honeymoon. But to make note of this bitterness is perhaps to get ahead of ourselves with regard to one of the elements of her unconscious strategy, an element that was to contribute to the formation of the symptom in this resentful wife. First we must follow the thread of the patient's discourse over the course of several sessions.

From the start the accent was on the reaction of surprise evoked by the husband's unexpected failing. This reaction would take on its full importance later in the story, if only because it seemed to have arisen as a genuine signal of anxiety. In other words, it was a defensive operation mobilized in the face of an impending psychic danger whose rush of excitation could have upset the equilibrium of the patient.

The afflux of excitation, originating in the prior registration of a experience of anxiety, must reach a threshold of alarm sufficient to alert the subject's defenses. It is in this sense that the surprise operated as an early warning sign of a past traumatic affect reactivated by the husband's present sexual failings. The symptom was to find its point of insertion in connection with this signal of anxiety.

At the outset, the reaction of surprise occurred as a defense against a number of immediate and local thoughts that were repressed on the spot. The analytic work revealed these thoughts one by one. First, there was the memory of a sexual potential that had to be painfully held in during the honeymoon. Then there was the identification of a violent hatred for the impotent husband. Finally, there was the recognition of the devastating narcissistic humiliation of having been incapable of arousing a man's desire. In the aftermath of the honeymoon, these various thoughts, at first repressed, became the object of a reversal of values through displacement. It was, indeed, in the form of the patient's mothering of her husband that the matter made its return. But at the same time as she was kindly consoling him, a symptom appeared that took the form of a writing disorder. Innocuous at first, this disorder quite rapidly became a constant, finally assuming the configuration of a rhythmical tremor of the arm that made the act of writing virtually impossible. Most of the time the appearance of this incomprehensible symptom was accompanied by a feeling of muted anger directed against herself, for which the patient could give no explanation.

As we shall see, this symptom was a genuine metaphoric construction, a signifying substitution of a new signifier for an old repressed one. The new signifier (the symptom) maintained a bond of similarity to the repressed signifier it replaced. Several months' worth of associations were necessary to identify this repressed signifier. The principal stages of the analytic work were marked by the recollection of a number of forgotten memories that played successive roles in the process of metaphorization.

First, the memory of an incident of no apparent importance: during their wedding night, the husband had accidentally spilled a glass of alcohol on the conjugal bed. Following this, the patient remembered an event from her adolescence. She had been asked to watch over a neighbor, who was having an attack of delirium tremens, until the doctor came. Lying on a bed, this man had flailed his arms about to repel a hallucinatory attack of vermin. She recalled how, terrified by the scene, she had been seized by a trembling that lasted until the arrival of the doctor.

Subsequently, and with great difficulty, she brought up several forgotten details of a traumatic event. Some time before her marriage, this woman had discovered that her father was really her stepfather. She was strongly affected by the discovery of this fact that had been hidden from her, and decided to try to find her father. Among the many investigations she undertook at the time there was one that she had totally forgotten. She now remembered having written to one of her father's old acquaintances. Since she had had great hopes of some results from this attempt, she was all the more frustrated when she had to wait a long time for an answer that never came. At last a final, fundamental memory emerged and catalyzed the preceding ones, yielding up the meaning of the symptom. This memory was like the last piece in the metaphoric puzzle. She remembered that one day, when she was 13 or 14 years old, her stepfather, who had had too much to drink, had harassed her by fondling her breasts insistently. Her immediate reaction had been one of great surprise, as this initiative was not habitual and was therefore unexpected. She also remembered the anger she felt toward herself when she realized that she was impotent in this situation. She had therefore waited in a state of anxiety for her stepfather to come to the end of his incestuous attentions.

These, then, were the principal memories in which certain signifiers played a major role in the metaphoric construction of the symptom. Let us look at them one by one as they appeared in the analysis:

1. *alcohol:* the glass of alcohol that was spilled on the bed
2. *the arm:* the flailing arm of the hallucinating alcoholic neighbor
3. *trembling:* the trembling of her body when she was with the delirious neighbor
4. *writing:* writing to her father's old acquaintance
5. *frustrating wait:* after having written the letter
6. *no answer:* to the letter
7. *great surprise:* when her stepfather fondled her breasts
8. *anger:* directed toward herself during the incestuous scene
9. *impotence:* inability to put an end to the scene
10. *anxious wait:* for the stepfather to stop his incestuous folly.

On the basis of these different elements we can easily understand the elective construction of the symptom. First, the patient's disappointment on her wedding night was the event that reactivated the repressed scene of incest. These two scenes share the same triggering element—the surprise effect—that, as we saw, functioned as a signal of anxiety in the wedding night episode by reactivating an anxiety-producing afflux of excitement. But this reactivation was possible only because of the *similarity of affect*: sexual arousal without libidinal discharge. In other words, a frustrating psychosexual tension was the underlying similarity in the two situations that prompted the organization of the symptom.

The symptom itself was structured like a metaphor. Let us call the incestuous scene with the stepfather $\frac{S1}{s1}$, and the writing symptom $\frac{S2}{s2}$. If we refer back to the structure of the metaphoric mechanism $\frac{S1}{s1} \longrightarrow \text{⑤②}$, we can understand how the symptom, as such, was the product of a signifying substitution for the repressed erotic excitement in the incest episode. The repetition of a similar trauma—the frustration of the wedding night—activated the process of substitution. But it is obvious that in the present case (and here is where it differs from the metaphoric mechanism as it functions in language) the similarity between the two signifying elements involved in the metaphor is not immediately apparent, and hence the symptom seems unintelligible. The similarity reveals itself only through the associations that produce the intermediary material necessary for the process of metaphoric substitution. This is what Lacan (1953b) means when he says that "the symptom resolves itself entirely in an analysis of language, because the symptom is itself structured like a language, [and] because it is from language that speech must be delivered" (p. 59).

Unconscious activity combines these diverse materials of different origin in such a way as to make the expression of the repressed desire unrecognizable. These materials that mark the organization of the symptom have certain common characteristics. For example, the signifier *alcohol* is explicitly or implicitly present in several of the forgotten memories: the glass of alcohol spilled on the marriage bed, the attack of delirium tremens, the drunken stepfather. It is the same for the signifier *waiting*: the husband drinks in bed instead of paying attention to the patient (frustrating wait), she must watch over the alcoholic neighbor while awaiting the arrival of the doctor (anxious wait), she waits in vain for an answer to her letter (frustrating wait), and finally she must wait for her stepfather to stop caressing her (anxious wait). All these elements of similarity suffice to precipitate the formation of the symptom. Its elaboration takes place by successive stratification, somewhat like the condensation process in dreams.

To see how this occurs, we have only to be attentive to the way in which this woman describes her symptom. She presents it as a rhythmical tremor of the arm that makes it almost impossible for her to write, which continually brings on feelings of anger. The traces of the different layers of stratification can be found in this description. The signifier *to write /writing* comes from one of the repressed memories. The rhythmical trembling of the arm represents the condensation of two elements from another forgotten memory, the shaking of the neighbor's arm during his zooptic hallucination, and the trembling of her own body when she witnessed this scene. Finally, the impossibility of writing and the subsequent anger repeat her own feelings of impotence when faced with her stepfather's caresses and the inner rage that accompanied these feelings. At the end of the primary-process activity that organizes and groups these different materials, we have the symptom (S2) that has been substituted for the incest scene (S1) in the manner of a metaphor.

One last word is needed, however, concerning an aspect of the repressed element $\frac{S1}{s1}$: the anger evoked by her impotence in the scene with the stepfather. This is a perfect example of a reversal of values, that is, of a metonymy/displacement. The anger she directs against herself is nothing other than the disguised reverse side of the unconscious experience. Above all, she is angry at her stepfather, in that the erotic excitement he aroused in her made her suffer because it was not brought to a less frustrating resolution. And the anxious impotence that prevented her from reacting expresses the opposite of the passive pleasure she obtained from the erotic advances of her stepfather. The expression of desire caused guilt only because the demands of the superego called for an immediate reversal of the value of the affects into their opposite. Thus passive waiting was all the more acceptable because it allowed for the expression of her desire while at the same time preserving morality thanks to a metonymic displacement.

It is easy to see how the conjugal failure on the wedding night might reactivate both passive excitement and frustration with the help of an identical kind of displacement. What happened, in effect, was that latent thoughts such as frustration, hatred for the husband, and narcissistic humiliation were quickly transformed into mothering tendencies. Why this metonymic reversal of the value of the affects? For one reason—to maintain in repression the incestuous scene with the stepfather that had been suddenly reactivated. The surest way to accomplish this was to introduce a reversal of the value of the affects that were evoked during the wedding night. In other words, the repetition of displacement with regard to the affects of the wedding night reinforced the displacement of the affects during the scene with the stepfather.

In sum, we find in this clinical fragment an illustration of the metaphoric construction of a symptom whose components have also been the object of metonymic displacements. More generally, as Lacan (1957) points out, the symptom is a return of the truth. It can be interpreted only in the order of the signifier, which has meaning only in its relation to another signifier. Likewise, "if the symptom is a metaphor, it is not a metaphor to say so. . . . For the symptom *is* a metaphor whether one likes it or not" (p. 175).

The symptom is thus an additional justification for the thesis that the unconscious is structured like a language. Now we will look at the mechanism that offers the most decisive confirmation of this thesis, the metaphor of the Name-of-the-Father.

Part II

The Paternal Metaphor as the Structural Crossroads of Subjectivity

11

The Predominance of the Phallus

Since the process of the paternal metaphor, the Name-of-the-Father, is the strongest argument for the thesis that the unconscious is structured like a language, before we look at it more closely a few preliminary remarks are necessary concerning the object that is central to it: *the phallic object*. These remarks are called for because the *phallus* is one of the most misused concepts in psychoanalytic commentaries, and because the phallic object is the keystone of Lacan's recentering of the problematics of the Oedipus complex and of castration within the context of the paternal metaphor.

First let us review what might be called the phallic problematic in Freud's thinking. Lacan's theoretical edifice rests largely on references to the phallic object, and in the perspective of the return to Freud he took pains to show how constant and central this reference is in Freud's work. His endeavor is clear from the time of the seminar on *The Psychoses* (1955–1956), especially in the following passages:

But ultimately, and I stress this, the pivot, the point of convergence of the libidinal dialectic that the mechanism and
development of neurosis refer to in Freud, is the theme of
castration. . . . Freud stuck by this predominance. In the
material, explanatory order of Freudian theory, from one end
to the other, it is a prevailing constant. He never subordi-
nated or even relativized its place in the theoretical process-
ing of the subjective interplay in which the history of any
psychoanalytic phenomenon whatsoever is inscribed. . . .
[I]n his work the phallic object occupies the central place
in the libidinal economy, for the man and for the woman.

   This is an altogether essential fact that characterizes all
the theorization presented and maintained by Freud. Whatever revisions he brought to his theorizing, throughout all
the phases of the schematization he presented of psychic life,
the predominance of the phallic center was never modified.
[p. 312, translation modified]

The paradox, Lacan notes, is that in spite of Freud's insis-
tence on this ongoing reference, the central and predominant
role of the phallic object has often been a source of major confusion, both for Freud's commentators and in analytic theory
in general. For Lacan, this confusion starts in the work of
one of Freud's first students, Ernest Jones, whose elaboration
of the concept of aphanisis may be seen as solid proof of the
misunderstanding that prevails regarding the question of the
phallus.

For Jones (1927), aphanisis refers to the disappearance of
sexual desire. This notion, articulated in connection with the
castration complex, expresses a fear more fundamental than that
of castration in men and women: "many men wish to be castrated
for, among others, erotic reasons, so that their sexuality certainly
does not disappear with the surrender of the penis" (pp. 439–

440). And Jones concludes that if the abolition of sexuality (aphanisis) and castration appear to be confused with one another, this is only because the fear of castration is never anything but a concrete expression of aphanisis.

For Lacan (1956–1957), this perfectly illustrates a misconception of the meaning and scope of the phallic object in Freud's work. First, Jones's concept of aphanisis is based on an implicit confusion between the penis and the phallus. In other words, this is a specific misrecognition of the nature of the phallic object, a nature that makes it possible for Freud to ascribe to this object a value and function that are identical for men and for women. Moreover, it is surely not by chance that Jones elaborates his notion of aphanisis in the context of his investigations in the field of feminine sexuality. According to him, the indicator of fear of aphanisis in women is the fear of separation from the loved object. Thus the common parameter of the sexuality of the little girl and the little boy antedates the castration complex. This proves that Jones does not agree that the libidinal evolution of the little girl is mobilized by castration and the predominance of the phallus. If her libidinal evolution must be centered on the same thing as for the boy, this central object is therefore not the phallus but aphanisis.

To put it in other terms, Lacan continues, Jones misses the very meaning of the reference to the phallic object. This is not a reference to castration via the penis, but a reference to the father, to a function that mediates the relationship of the child to the mother, the mother to the child. Moreover, Jones's confusion also stems from the fact that he is not clear about the nature of the lack of the object. Essentially, he makes no rigorous distinction between *privation* and *castration*. He refers to a category of lack of object that he calls castration but that is, in fact, only privation. (The modalities of the lack of the object and the distinctions among privation, frustration, and castration will be discussed in Chapter 12.)

One could mention many similar confusions in psychoanalytic thought. Nonetheless, we should not lose sight of the fact that, even if this phallic reference is prevalent in Freud's work, it is very often implicit, and as such it metaphorizes the subjective status of the phallic object. The subject never stops trying to justify his possession of it; at the same time he assiduously claims that he does not have it—when, in the end, no one has it. That Freud's phallic references, while numerous, are mostly implicit can be accounted for by the underlying mechanism that makes the phallic reference operative, namely what Lacan (1955–1956) calls the paternal function.

> As for his perspective, Freud never completely elucidated it, but it's what makes his position tenable with regard to this kind of reduction to a plan, or a single plane, of instinctual signs to which, after him, psychoanalytic dynamics have tended to be reduced. I'm speaking of those terms that he never abandoned, that he requires for any possible psychoanalytic understanding, even where it hangs together only approximately, since it hangs together all the better in this way—namely, the function of the father and the Oedipus complex.
>
> It can't be a question purely and simply of imaginary elements. What we find in the imaginary[1] in the form of the phallic mother isn't homogeneous, as you're all aware, with

---

1. Translator's note: According to the author (personal communication), "*The imaginary*, a term that underwent important modifications in Lacan's work, refers here to the representation of a mother who is not lacking, that is to say, a mother who is assumed to be unconditionally fulfilled by her child, the child being identified with the object of her lack, the phallus."

the castration complex insofar as the latter is integrated into the triangular situation of the Oedipus complex. This situation is not completely elucidated by Freud, but by virtue of the sole fact that it is always maintained it is there ready to lend itself to elucidation, which is possible only if we recognize that the third person, central for Freud, that is, the father, has a signifying element that is irreducible to any kind of imaginary conditioning. [pp. 315–316, translation modified]

In other words, it is clear on the basis of Freud's work itself that the phallus is not the penis attributed, on the level of the imaginary order, to the woman as phallic mother, but that, on the contrary, the father is structurally the third element in the oedipal situation only because the phallus is the *signifying element* that is attributed to him. This is the first point of our definition: *the phallic object is above all an object whose nature it is to be a signifying element.*

It must be admitted that this signifying identity of the phallic object is not easily accessible in Freud's work, in that the very term *phallus* is notably absent in his writings. As Laplanche and Pontalis (1973) note, Freud mostly uses the adjective "phallic" to characterize the object (phallic organization, phallic stage, phallic mother). However, every time the term "phallic" appears it is in reference to a symbolic function. Even if, originally, the elaboration of the concept of the phallic object is in a way based on the anatomical reality of the penis, it is clear that for Freud the function attributed to such an object could never be reduced to the circumstance of having or not having a penis. So if the phallus is predominant, it is so only as a symbolic referent.

Freud had his first intuition of the primacy of the phallus as early as 1905 in "Three essays on the theory of sexuality"; it is explicitly discussed in "The infantile genital organization," which Freud offered in 1923 as a complement to "Three Essays."

In this later text, the predominance of the phallus is linked to the problematic of castration in the following way:

> [T]he main characteristic of this 'infantile genital organization' is its *difference* from the final genital organization of the adult. This consists in the fact that, for both sexes, only one genital, namely the male one, comes into account. What is present, therefore, is not a primacy of the genitals, but a primacy of the *phallus*. [Freud 1923, p. 142]

The fact that the essential role of only one genital organ is recognized at a certain stage in infantile sexual development implies that this primacy, from the outset, is not located in the realm of anatomical reality or on the level of organs, but precisely on the level of what a lack of the organ might represent subjectively.

Freud (1923) makes the same radical distinction by linking castration to the phallic order and not to the penis.

> The *lack of a penis* [my italics] is regarded as a result of castration, and so now the child is faced with the task of coming to terms with castration in relation to himself. The further developments are too well known generally to make it necessary to recapitulate them here. But it seems to me that *the significance of the castration complex can only be rightly appreciated if its origin in the phase of phallic primacy is also taken into account.* [Freud's italics] [p. 144]

The arguments Freud deploys in this text exactly describe the nature of the phallic object. First there is the notion of lack (the lack of a penis) leading to the preferment of the phallic object and, in so doing, locating it unambiguously in a dimension beyond that of anatomical reality. In fact, sexual difference is constituted from the outset on the basis of this notion of lack:

the feminine genital organ is different from the masculine one only because it lacks something. In addition, the product of observation (perceptual reality) is immediately elaborated on the subjective level as a conception: Freud writes "the lack of a penis is *regarded as.*" This conception of something lacking inevitably assigns what is thought to be lacking to the only place possible for it, the imaginary order.

In other words, the child broaches the question of sexual difference with the following sort of psychic logic: Why make things simple when they can be complicated? In fact, the reality of the sexes requires that they be anatomically different. But what we observe is that the child's psyche elaborates on this reality, creating a construction in which the difference is subjected to the order of lack. In other words, it is—and it is only—because the child persists in thinking there is something missing that the sexes become differentiated for him. This imaginary construction, imperatively summoning up the idea of a lack in the face of the reality of the difference between the sexes, implicitly postulates the existence of *an object that is likewise imaginary: the phallus.* This imaginary object provides total support for the child's fantasy when he tries to conceive of something *lacking* that he imagines should be there.

The imaginary nature of the phallus thus dictates a certain profile for the problematics of castration. As Freud (1923) puts it, this lack confronts the child "with the task of coming to terms with castration in relation to himself" (p. 144). We are not, of course, talking about a personal confrontation with castration. The difference may be trivial, but what we note in Freud's formulation is the exteriority attributed to castration, echoing the exteriority of the phallic object itself. This exteriority is intrasubjective, however, since it concerns the subject's relationship with an intrapsychic formation, the fantasy, whose substance is

purely imaginary. It remains the case that, underlying the problematics of the phallus that are anchored in the imaginary order,
there is also a symbolic dimension that leads us directly to the
paternal metaphor. In other words, the primacy of the phallus
as imaginary object plays a fundamental structuring role in the
oedipal dialectic, in that the phallic dynamic itself inaugurates
a symbolic operation that is resolved in the advent of the metaphor of the Name-of-the-Father.

It is in the domain of these Freudian references that Lacan
systematizes the problematics of the phallus as foundational to
psychoanalytic theory. Specifically, Lacan establishes the phallus as the primordial signifier of desire in oedipal triangulation.
The Oedipus complex plays itself out around locating the position of the phallus in relation to the desire of the mother, the
child, and the father. A dialectical process develops in two modes:
that of *being the phallus* and that of *having the phallus*.

The process of the paternal metaphor is structurally linked
to the oedipal situation, as it were constituting its resolutory
culmination. Lacan's theoretical exposition of the Oedipus complex stresses the recentering of its meaning in the only register
in which Freudian theory shows it to be intelligible. This register not only belongs to the realm of imaginary capture (to be
discussed in the next chapter) but also has an nodal point where
the imaginary capture is fastened to the symbolic dimension.

By its participation in the imaginary register, it appears that,
as Lacan (1953a) observes, "the Oedipus complex, in which
analytic theory concretizes the intersubjective relationship, has
a mythical value" (p. 292). On the other hand, because the
oedipal process requires this intersubjective relation to find a
point of assumption into the symbolic order, it contributes to
the structuring of the subject. Without these nodal references
to the imaginary and symbolic orders, the Oedipus complex is

caught in the net of psychological ideology. Most of the polemics and misunderstandings surrounding this complex seem to be rooted in this ideological obtuseness. Conversely, as soon as the oedipal process is recentered around the double reference to the imaginary and symbolic orders, most of the objections to it collapse.

12

The Mirror Stage and the Oedipus Complex

This space in which the Oedipus complex becomes intelligible was defined by Lacan (1957–1958) around the metaphor of the Name-of-the-Father, a process whose main function is to link the *phallic function* to its correlate, the *castration complex*.[1] The operator that negotiates this connection is the signifier Name-of-the-Father, which marks out and structures the entire Oedipal trajectory.

More generally, Lacan's view is that the basic function of the Oedipal process is coextensive with the *paternal function*.[2]

---

1. "This structure, which we have put forth here as being that of metaphor, contains all the possibilities for a clear articulation of the Oedipus complex and its motivation, the castration complex. Castration, therefore—insofar as on the one hand it is profoundly linked to the symbolic articulation of the incest taboo, and on the other hand (and in the forefront of our experience, even more so for those who are the special objects of our experience, namely neurotics) is something that manifests itself on the imaginary level" (Lacan 1957–1958, seminar of January 22, 1958).

2. "There is no question of the Oedipus complex if there is no father; conversely, to speak of the Oedipus complex is to introduce the function of the father as essential" (seminar of January 15, 1958).

This function is to be understood as something radically distinct from the actual presence of the father[3] or from negative occurrences such as his absence, deficiency, or any other form of personal inconsistency on his part.[4] For Lacan, this function proceeds from the determination of a place, at the same time as this place gives it a necessarily symbolic dimension. In addition, since it is a symbolic function, it lends itself to a metaphoric operation. That is why Lacan (1957–1958) is justified in examining the paternal function in these terms:

> The father is not a real object, so what is he? . . . The father is a metaphor.
> What is a metaphor? . . . It's a signifier that takes the place of another signifier. . . . The father is a signifier substituted for another signifier. And this is the province and the only essential province of the father as he intervenes in the Oedipus complex. [seminar of January 15, 1958]

---

3. "Can an Oedipus complex be normally constituted when there is no father? . . . We've noticed that it wasn't all that simple, that an Oedipus complex might very well be constituted even when the father wasn't there. . . . Oedipus complexes that are completely normal—normal in both senses: normalizing, on the one hand, and also normal in terms of how they denormalize, I mean by their neuroticizing effects, for example—are established in exactly the same way as in other cases, even in cases where the father isn't there" (seminar of January 15, 1958).

4. "As far as deficiency is concerned, I would simply like to call to your attention that when the father has shortcomings, and insofar as we speak of shortcomings, we never know in what respect . . . . We began to see the problem of his deficiency, not directly, . . . but, as was clear from the outset, it is as a member of the fundamental trio, the familial ternary, that is to say, insofar as he takes his place in the family, that we could start to say a few somewhat more effective things about his shortcomings. . . . To speak of his deficiency in the family is not the same as to speak of his deficiency in the complex. Because to speak of his deficiency in the complex, a dimension other than the dimension of reality must be introduced" (seminar of January 15, 1958).

Lacan (1949) situates the onset of the Oedipus complex at a specific threshold of the child's maturation, corresponding to a particular phase of psychic experience. This phase is contemporary with the *mirror stage*, during which a certain type of identification begins to take shape against a background of alienation specific to the relation with the mother.

THE MIRROR STAGE

The mirror stage is organized around a fundamental experience of identification in the course of which the child becomes master of his own body image. The child's primary identification with this image promotes the structuring of the "I" and puts an end to that singular aspect of psychic experience that Lacan calls *the fantasy of the fragmented body*. For in fact, before the mirror stage, the child does not yet experience his body as a unified totality but as something disjointed. The mirror dialectic puts to the test this fantasy experience of the fragmented body, vestiges of which reappear in certain dreams and in the processes of psychotic breakdown. Its function is to neutralize the frightening dispersion in favor of the unity of one's own body:

> The *mirror stage* is a drama whose internal thrust hastens forward from insufficiency to anticipation—and which contrives for the subject, caught up in the lure of spatial identification, the succession of fantasies that extend from a fragmented body-image to a form of its totality that I shall call orthopedic. . . . [Lacan 1949, p. 4, translation modified]

The child's experience in the mirror stage is divided into three fundamental periods that mark the progressive conquest of his body image. At first, it is as if the child perceives the image of his body in the mirror as a real being, one that he tries to approach or take hold of. This phase of the experience, in other words, indicates an *initial confusion between self and other*, a confusion amply confirmed by the stereotyped relations he has with other children. These relations unequivocally confirm that it is primarily through the other that he experiences himself and orients himself at first:

> It is this captation by the *imago* of the human form . . . which, between the ages of six months and two and a half years, dominates the entire dialectic of the child's behavior in the presence of his counterparts. During the whole of this period, we note the emotional reactions and the spoken accounts of a normal transitivism. The child who strikes another says he has been struck; the child who sees another fall, cries. [Lacan 1948, p. 19, translation modified]

If this first period of the mirror stage clearly reveals the child's subjection to the imaginary register, the second constitutes a decisive step in the process of identification. The child is surreptitiously led to discover that the other in the mirror is not a real being, but only an image. He no longer tries to grab hold of it, and, what is more, his behavior in general indicates that he now knows how to distinguish the image of the other from the reality of the other.

The third period transforms the first two into a dialectic, not only because the child becomes certain that the mirror reflection is an image, but above all because he acquires the conviction that this image is his own. In *re-cognizing* himself through the image, he is able to reassemble the scattered, fragmented body into a unified totality, the representation of his own body. The body image is therefore a structuring factor in the formation of the subject's identity, since it is through this image that he achieves his primal identification.

The entire process of this conquest of identity is grounded in the imaginary dimension, in that the child identifies himself through something virtual (the optical image) that is not himself but something through which he nonetheless re-cognizes himself. What we are dealing with, then, is an *imaginary recognition*, which is also justified by objective facts. For at the age when this takes place, the child is not yet mature enough to have a specific *cognition* of his own body: the experience of the mirror stage is prior to the advent of the body schema.[5] But although the mirror phase symbolizes the "preformation" of the "I," it presupposes by its fundamental nature the destiny of the "I" as alienated in the imaginary dimension. The re-cognition of the self in the mirror image is accomplished—for optical reasons— through indications that are exterior and symmetrically inverted. At the same time, therefore, the very unity of the body takes form as exterior to the self and inverted. And so this re-cognition in itself prefigures, for the subject who is in the process of acquiring his identity, the nature of his imaginary alienation and the beginnings of the chronic misrecognition that will characterize all his future relations with himself.

THE FIRST PHASE OF THE OEDIPUS COMPLEX

At the end of the identificatory phase of the mirror stage, the child has begun his development as a subject but is still in a quasi-fusional relationship of undifferentiation with the mother. This

---

5. "I believed that I myself could show that on such occasions the child anticipates on the mental plane the conquest of the functional unity of his own body, which, at that stage, is still incomplete on the plane of voluntary motility. What we have there is a first captation by the image in which the first stage of the dialectic of identifications can be discerned" (Lacan 1948, p. 18).

relation is the result of a particular position taken by the child toward his mother as he seeks *to identify with what he supposes to be the object of her desire.* This identification, through which *the desire of the child becomes desire of the desire of the mother,* is to a great extent facilitated, even induced, by the mother's unmediated closeness to the child, even if only for caretaking and the satisfaction of basic needs. In other words, the closeness of these exchanges leads the child to take himself to be the object that the mother supposedly lacks. This object that is capable of filling in the lack in the other[6] is the *phallus.* In his relation to the mother the child therefore encounters the problematics of the phallus in the form of his desire to become the maternal phallus. In this sense we can speak of a kind of fusional undifferentiation between mother and child from the time when the child identifies himself with the one and only object of the other's desire. As Lacan notes, in this first phase of the oedipal process the child's desire remains radically subjected to that of the mother.

> What the child wants is to become the desire of desire, to be able to satisfy the mother's desire, that is, "to be or not to be" the object of the mother's desire. . . . To please the mother . . . it is necessary and sufficient to be the phallus.[7] [Lacan 1957–1958, seminar of January 22, 1958]

It is one thing to say, as Lacan does in this seminar, that "the relation of the child to the phallus is essential as long as the phallus is the object of the mother's desire." He takes things a step further by saying that at this stage the child is clearly re-

---

6. Here it is a question of the "*o*ther" taken for the "*O*ther," as we shall see later.

7. Translator's note: The words "to be or not to be" appear in English in the original.

moved from the phallic problematic by virtue of the *dialectic of being*: to be or not to be the phallus. In this first oedipal period, then, it is as if the child spares himself one of the fundamental contingencies of the phallic problematic, the dimension of castration. Indeed, a fusional relation with the mother can exist only to the extent that *it seems as if* no third element is mediating the child's phallic identification with her. But, conversely, the very nature of the phallic object with which the child identifies indicates the radically imaginary aspect of this conviction. Therefore, even if the mediating agency (the father) is seen as foreign to the mother–child relation, the child's phallic identification itself presupposes that agency's existence. In short, the identification with the phallic object that eludes the mediation of castration calls it forth all the more in the form of a dialectical oscillation between *being and not being the phallus*.

The emergence of such an oscillation marks the beginning of the second phase of the Oedipus complex, in which the child is inescapably brought into the register of castration as the paternal dimension imposes itself. The child's evolution in the mysteries of the oedipal process may become fixated at a point of unstable equilibrium regarding what is at stake in the question: to be or not to be the phallus. If this question is left unresolved as a result of an equivocal message concerning the symbolic function of the father, there will be a perpetual oscillation with regard to castration, and "a certain number of disorders and disturbances can become established, among which are those identifications that we have characterized as 'perverse'" (Lacan 1957–1958, seminar of January 22, 1958).

A sustained ambiguity on this level will lead the child to institute a defensive strategy in order to avoid castration. But the pervert does not deceive himself about the subjective position that binds him to the predominance of the phallus on the level of the imaginary. Because he accurately assesses the impact of castration, he is all the more adept at cultivating the paradoxical singularity of his position in relation to it. All the ingenuity of his symptoms—and all his anxiety—will revolve around reproducing and maintaining the subjective delusion in which he is caught. He must constantly sense all the ways in which castration might occur if he wishes to exercise the maximum of skill in getting around it. In other words, perverse identification brings up in negative form the two related questions of the mother's privation of her phallic object and the child's detachment from his identification with this object. These are precisely the intersubjective stakes involved in the second structuring phase of the Oedipus complex.

THE SECOND PHASE OF THE OEDIPUS COMPLEX

The mediation of the father plays a leading role in configuring the mother–child–phallus relation. He intervenes in the form of *privation*:

> Experience has proven that the father, insofar as he *deprives* the mother of this object, namely of the phallic object, of her desire, plays an absolutely essential role in . . . the entire course of the Oedipus complex, even in the easiest and most normal cases. [Lacan 1957–1958, seminar of January 22, 1958, emphasis added]

What is more, the intrusion of the paternal presence is experienced by the child as a *prohibition* and a *frustration*:

> The father shows up here nonetheless as a nuisance. He is not only cumbersome because of his size; he is in the posi-

tion of troublemaker because of what he *prohibits*. What does
he prohibit? . . . First, he forbids the satisfaction of the impulse. . . .

What else does the father prohibit? Well, this is where
we started out: since the mother belongs to him she doesn't
belong to the child. . . . The father well and truly *frustrates*
the child where the mother is concerned. [Lacan 1957–1958,
seminar of January 15, 1958]

In other words, the father's intrusion into the mother–
child–phallus relation manifests itself in three apparently different registers: *prohibition, frustration*, and *privation*. Things get
more complicated when it becomes apparent that the combined
activity of this prohibiting, frustrating, depriving father tends
to catalyze his basic function as *castrating* father.

The Lack of the Object

A review of the concept of the *lack of the object* according to Lacan
(1956–1957) will help us in our understanding of the dynamics
of the second phase of the Oedipus complex. In the child as in
the adult, the lack of the object can appear in three specific
modes: frustration, privation, and castration. In each of these
three cases there is lack of the object, but in each case the nature of the lack is qualitatively different. The same is true of the
type of object in question.

Frustration is, preeminently, the realm of the demand or
claim, except that there can never be any possibility of obtain-
ing satisfaction. Indeed, in the case of frustration the lack takes
the form of imaginary harm. The object of the frustration, however, is itself entirely real. The penis is the prototype of such an
object, and it is certainly with frustration that the little girl ex-

periences its absence. More generally, the child experiences the mother's lack of a penis as a frustration.

In *privation*, on the other hand, it is the lack that is real. Lacan designates this type of lack as a hole in the real. But the object of privation is a symbolic object.

Finally, in *castration*, the lack involved is symbolic, since it concerns the incest taboo, the symbolic reference *par excellence*. It is this that makes the paternal function operative in governing the child's access to the symbolic order. The lack signified by castration is above all, as Lacan puts it, a *symbolic debt*. But in castration the object that is lacking is radically imaginary and can never be a real object. This imaginary object of castration is, of course, the phallus.

The ordering and interconnections of these different categories of lack and their different objects can be visualized on this mnemonic schema, designed by Jean Oury:

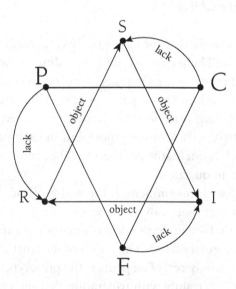

Its construction is simple:

1. Draw a Star of David
2. Proceeding clockwise, place the following initials at the points of each triangle:
   PCF (Privation—Castration—Frustration)
   SIR (Symbolic—Imaginary—Real)

The categories of lack and their corresponding objects may be decoded by following the arrows counterclockwise:

—castration is the symbolic lack of an imaginary object
—frustration is the imaginary lack of a real object
—privation is the real lack of a symbolic object

Now let us come back to the second phase of the Oedipus complex, which begins with the paternal intrusion into the inter-subjective mother–child relationship. This intrusion has two aspects. From the child's point of view, the father intervenes with a prohibition as he presents himself as the rightful claimant to the mother. This is why his intervention is experienced by the child as "a *frustration*, an imaginary act concerning a very real object, the mother, insofar as the child needs her" (Lacan 1957–1958, seminar of January 15, 1958). The child is thus required to reassess his phallic identification and, at the same time, to give up being the object of the mother's desire. Correspondingly, from the mother's point of view, the father *deprives* her of the phallus she presumably has in the form of the child identified with the object of her desire:

It is thus on the level of the *privation* of the mother that, at a given point in Oedipal development, the subject faces the question of accepting, registering, symbolizing himself, and rendering meaningful this privation of which the mother proves to be the object. . . . What is the special configuration of this relationship to the mother, to the father, to the phallus that makes it impossible for the child to accept that the mother is *deprived* by the father of something that is the object of her desire? . . . This is a nodal configuration. On this level, the question that presents itself is *"to be or not to be" the phallus.*[8] [Lacan 1957–1958, seminar of January 22, 1958, emphasis added]

The origin of the child's oscillation in this dialectic of being that concerns both frustration and privation is the fundamental fact that the father appears as an *other* with regard to the mother–child relationship. As such, in the child's subjective experience, he emerges as a possible object of the mother's desire, a possible phallic object that the child might suppose to be a rival in his relation with her. The stakes of this imaginary rivalry are, in reality, coextensive with a displacement of the phallic object that leads the child to an encounter with the *law of the father.*

The child is confronted with this law when he discovers that the mother is herself dependent on it with regard to her ability to satisfy the child's demands. In other words, it is through the mother that the desire of the child inevitably encounters the law of the other.

In the imaginary dimension the father most certainly intervenes as the depriver of the mother, that is to say that what is addressed to the other as a demand is referred to a higher

---

8. Translator's note: The words "to be or not to be" are in English in the original.

court, is relayed as it should be, because, in certain respects, the question we put to "the other," if he considers it in its entirety, always encounters this other's "other," namely his own law. And it is on this level that something happens that makes it so that what comes back to the child is purely and simply the law of the father insofar as it is imaginarily conceived by the subject as depriving the mother. [Lacan 1957–1958, seminar of January 22, 1958]

Thus the child discovers the most essential dimension in the structuring of desire to be that which submits everyone's desire to the law of the desire of the other. For the child, this powerful moment of the Oedipus complex channels the meaning of the mother's desire with regard to what he had up to now supposed to be its object. The fact that the mother's desire is subjected to the law of the desire of the other implies that her desire is itself dependent upon an object that the other (the father) is presumed to have or not to have. The *dialectic of having* (having the phallus or not having it) that the child discovers as, from here on, polarizing the problematics of the mother's desire, thus becomes the counterpart of the *dialectic of being* that regulates his experience of his own desire.

The child arrives at this self-questioning—to be or not to be the mother's phallus—only to the extent that the depriving father gives him to understand that the mother recognizes the paternal law as mediating her desire for an object that is no longer the child, but is something the father presumably has or does not have. According to Lacan (1957–1958), this is the stage where

something that detaches the subject from his identification simultaneously attaches him to the first appearance of the law in the form of the fact that the mother is dependent on

it, dependent on an object, an object that is no longer simply the object of her desire, but an object that the other has
or doesn't have. [seminar of January 22, 1958]

And he adds:

The tight link between this referral of the mother to a law
that is not her own and the fact that in reality the object of
her desire is "supremely" possessed by this same "other" to
whose law she refers: here we have the key to the Oedipal
relation and what makes the nature of the mother's relation
so essential, so decisive as a relation—and please do make
this distinction—not to the father, but to the word [*parole*]
of the father. . . .

Because he is a presence that deprives, it is he who bears
the law, and this is done in a way that is not veiled but is
mediated by the mother who puts him in the position of lawmaker. [seminar of January 22, 1958]

The second oedipal phase is the indispensable precondition
for the child's gaining access to the symbolization of the law that
marks the waning of the Oedipus complex. In this encounter
with the law of the father, the child is confronted with the question of *castration*, which challenges him through the "dialectic
of having" on which, henceforth, his mother's desire depends.
As a result of the father's mediation with regard to the mother,
who recognizes him as her lawmaker, the child promotes the
father to a position where he must appear as the guardian of the
phallus.

The real father is a "representative" of the law. As he is now
presumed to possess the object of the mother's desire, the child
invests him with a new meaning: he is elevated to the rank of

symbolic father. The mother, complying with the utterance of the paternal law by recognizing the word of the father[9] as being the only one that can mobilize her desire, also participates in giving a symbolic dimension to the function of the father in the child's eyes. At this point the child has to determine his own position vis-à-vis the father's signifying function. This function is the symbolic signifier known as the *Name-of-the-Father*.

> In other words, the relation in which the mother establishes the father as mediator of something that is beyond her law and her whim, and that is purely and simply the law as such, the father, therefore, as Name-of-the-Father, that is to say, as any development of Freudian theory announces and advances it, namely as closely linked to that enunciation of the law—this is what is essential, and it is in this that the relation is accepted or not accepted by the child, who deprives or does not deprive the mother of the object of her desire. [Lacan 1957–1958, seminar of January 22, 1958]

The positioning of the child at the end of this second oedipal phase is crucial, in the sense that it is primarily a positioning in relation to the phallic object. His certainty that he himself is the phallic object desired by the mother has been shaken. From now on, the paternal function forces the child not only to accept that he is not the phallus, but also to accept that he, like

---

9. "It is thus here that this 'other' to whom he [the child] addresses himself, namely, the mother . . . has a certain relation that is a relation to the father. . . . It is not so much a question of the personal relationship between the father and the mother . . . as it is, strictly speaking, a stage that must be experienced as such and that concerns the relations not simply of the person of the mother with the person of the father, but of the mother with *the word of the father*" (Lacan 1957–1958, seminar of January 22, 1958, emphasis added).

the mother, does not have it. He realizes that she desires it in the place where it presumably is, and where, therefore, it is now possible to have it. This is where we find the effect of the *castration complex*. Lacan (1957–1958) explains that it would not be so named

> if in a certain way it didn't emphasize that to have it [the phallus], it is first necessary to grant that one cannot have it, that this possibility of being castrated is essential in the assumption of the fact of having the phallus. This is the step that must be taken, this is where, at some point, effectively, in reality, actually, the father must intervene. [seminar of January 22, 1958]

This step that must be taken in the conquest of the phallus appears in a third phase that establishes a dialectic between the two preceding ones.

THE THIRD PHASE OF THE OEDIPUS COMPLEX

This is the period of "the waning of the Oedipus complex." It ends the phallic rivalry for the mother in which the child has placed himself and, imaginarily, the father. Once the father is invested with the phallic attribute, he must "prove it," as Lacan (1957–1958) says, since

> it is insofar as he intervenes in the third stage as the one who has the phallus, and not the one who is it, that something can occur that reestablishes the agency of the phallus as the object of the mother's desire, and not just as an object of which the father can deprive her. [seminar of January 22, 1958]

The high point of this stage is the *symbolization of the law*, attesting to the fact that the child has caught its full meaning. The structuring value of this symbolization lies in the child's locating the exact place of the mother's desire, and it is only under this condition that the paternal function represents the law. The child's encounter with the phallic relation is decisively altered in the sense that he leaves the problematics of being the phallus and accepts that he must cope with the problematics of having it. This occurs only to the extent that the father no longer appears to the child as a rival phallus in relation to the mother. Insofar as he *has* the phallus, the father is no longer the one who deprives the mother of the object of her desire. On the contrary, because he is presumed to be the possessor of the phallus, he restores it to the only place where it can be desired by the mother. The child then, like the mother, finds himself inscribed in the dialectic of having: the mother who does not have the phallus can desire it in the one who possesses it; the child, who is likewise deprived of it, can covet it where it can be found.

The dialectic of having inevitably calls forth a play of identifications. Boys and girls are inscribed differently in the logic of identifications that is activated by phallic issues. The boy who gives up the idea of being the maternal phallus enters into the dialectic of having by identifying with the father, who is presumed to have the phallus. The girl, too, can move away from the position of being the object of the mother's desire and can enter the dialectic of having by not having the phallus. She thereby finds it possible to identify with the mother, since, like the mother, "she knows where it is, she knows where she must go to get it, that is, to the father, to the one who has it" (Lacan 1957–1958, seminar of January 22, 1958).

The positioning of the phallus is a structuring element for the child of either sex once the father, who is presumed to have

it, becomes the object of the mother's preference. This preference bears witness to the passage from the register of being to
the register of having. It is the clearest proof of *the establishment
of the process of the paternal metaphor* and of its corresponding
intrapsychic mechanism, *primal repression.*

13

The Paternal Metaphor—
The Name-of-the-Father—
The Metonymy of Desire

The *fort-da* game described by Freud in *Beyond the Pleasure Principle* (1920) is without a doubt the clearest illustration of the way in which the child, as he accedes to the symbolic order, achieves the metaphor of the Name-of-the-Father, or *symbolic mastery of the lost object*:

> One day I made an observation which confirmed my view. The child had a wooden reel with a piece of string tied round it. It never occurred to him to pull it along the floor behind him, for instance, and play at its being a carriage. What he did was to hold the reel by the string and very skillfully throw it over the edge of his curtained cot, so that it disappeared into it, at the same time uttering his expressive "o-o-o-o" [for German *fort*, "gone"]. He then pulled the reel out of the cot again by the string and hailed its reappearance with a joyful "*da*" ["there"]. This, then, was the complete game—disappearance and return. As a rule one only witnessed its first act, which was repeated untiringly as a game in itself, though there is no doubt that the greater pleasure was attached to the second act. [p. 15]

And he continues:

> The interpretation of the game then became obvious. It was
> related to the child's great cultural achievement—the in-
> stinctual renunciation (that is, the renunciation of instinc-
> tual satisfaction) which he had made in allowing his mother
> to go away without protesting. He compensated himself for
> this, as it were, by himself staging the disappearance and
> return of the objects within his reach. [p. 15]

It would be hard to find a more exact illustration of the
Lacanian expression *signifying substitution*. The *fort-da* involves
a double metaphoric process. The reel is a metaphor for the
mother; the play between presence and absence is also metaphoric, symbolizing her comings and goings. In addition, the
child's playful activity—and this is the most instructive part of
Freud's observation—proves that he has turned the situation
completely to his advantage:

> On an unprejudiced view one gets an impression that the
> child turned his experience into a game from another
> motive. At the outset he was in a *passive* situation—he was
> overpowered by the experience; but, by repeating it, un-
> pleasurable though it was, as a game, he took on an *active*
> part. [p. 16]

The child has indeed turned the situation around: from now
on, it is he who leaves his mother, *symbolically*. This symbolic
reversal is the most obvious proof that an act of mastery has
occurred; the child has *mastered absence* through an identification. The mother had rejected him by leaving. Now he rejects
her by pushing away the reel, and so he is overjoyed when he
discovers his control over the absence of the lost object, the

mother. In other words, the *fort-da* demonstrates that the child has truly mastered the fact that he is not the one and only object of his mother's desire, that is, *the object that fills the lack in the Other (the phallus).* He can now mobilize his desire as *desire of a subject* towards objects that substitute for the lost one. But, above all, it is the advent of language (accession to the symbolic register) that is the incontestable sign of symbolic mastery of the lost object through the achievement of the paternal metaphor, an achievement based on *primal repression.*

Primal repression is a fundamental structuring process of metaphorization, the very act of primordial symbolization of the Law. It is accomplished by the *substitution of the paternal signifier for the phallic signifier.*

What does this symbolization imply? First, the subjective experience in which the child frees himself from an immediate experience and finds a substitute for it. This is the meaning of Lacan's formula "the thing must be lost in order to be represented." The child's immediate experience is based on the terms of his captivity in the *dialectic of being*—being the sole object of mother's desire, being the object that fills in her lack, being her phallus. In order to substitute something else for this experience in the mode of *being,* the child must gain access to the dimension of *having.* But making this dialectical move presupposes that the child is able to distinguish himself both from his immediate experience and from the symbolic substitute he calls forth to represent it. In other words, this process requires that the child position himself as *subject* and no longer only as *object* of the desire of the Other. The advent of this subject occurs through an inaugural operation of language in which the child strives to designate symbolically his renunciation of the lost object. Symbolic designation is possible only on the basis of the *repression of the phallic signifier, the signifier of the mother's desire.* Let us call this signifier, the one that governs the subsequent network composed of the entire chain of signifiers, S1:

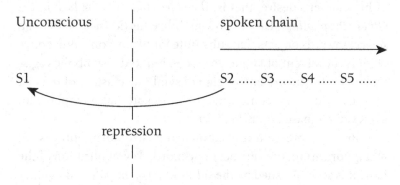

Primal repression is thus an intrapsychic operation that ensures the passage from immediately experienced reality to its symbolization in language. To understand how primal repression establishes access to the paternal metaphor, let us take another look at the formula for metaphoric substitution:

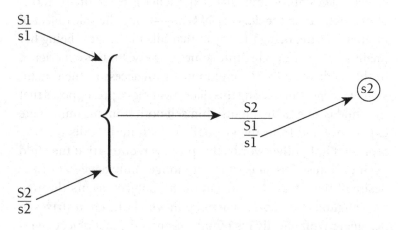

The metaphoric process consists in introducing a new signifier (S2) that pushes the former signifier (S1) under the bar

of signification in such a way as to keep it temporarily unconscious. Lacan schematizes this substitution with the following
algorithm:

$$\frac{S2}{\cancel{S}1} \cdot \frac{\cancel{S}1}{x} \longrightarrow S2\left(\frac{U}{x}\right)$$

The process here is that of the *fort-da* experience, where the
child tries out the renunciation of the way he formerly expressed
his desire as he now alternates the absences and presences of
his mother:

> What *does* she want? I'd like it to be me that she wants, but
> it's clear that it's not just me; there's something else on her
> mind. What's on her mind is the x, the signified. The signi-
> fied of the mother's comings and goings is the phallus. [Lacan
> 1957–1958, seminar of January 15, 1958]

Let us designate the expression of this original desire as follows:

$$\frac{S1}{s1} \Longleftrightarrow \frac{\text{Signifier of the mother's desire}}{\text{Idea of the mother's desire: phallus}}$$

As we have seen, at a given point in oedipal development
the child comes to associate the absence of his mother with the
presence of his father. Whenever she is away from him, the child
assumes that she is with the father. This is, once again, the crucial phase when the father appears to the child first as a rival
phallic object, and then as the one who is presumed to possess
the phallus. The child thus works out a signifying relation as
soon as he is able to *designate/name* the cause of his mother's
absences by summoning up the exemplar of the Father who has
the phallus, the *symbolic father*. In other words, it is here that the
Name-of-the-Father appears specifically in association with the
symbolic Law it embodies. The Name-of-the-Father designates

the recognition of a symbolic function defined in the place from which the law exercises its influence. This designation is the product of a metaphor, the Name-of-the-Father being the new signifier (S2) that, for the child, is substituted for the signifier of the desire of the mother:

> The function of the father in the Oedipus complex is to be a signifier substituted for a signifier, that is, for the first signifier introduced in symbolization, the maternal signifier. . . . It is to the extent that the father—in the formula for metaphor that I set out for you on a previous occasion—that he takes the place of the mother (S substituted for S'), the mother having already been linked to an x, that is, to something that was the signified in the mother–child relation. [Lacan 1957–1958, seminar of January 15, 1958]

In the course of the signifying substitution, the signifier of the desire of the mother, S1, thus becomes the object of repression (primal repression) and becomes unconscious. As Lacan (1957–1958) puts it, "it is insofar as the father is substituted for the mother as signifier that the usual result of the metaphor is produced, the result that is expressed in the following formula" (seminar of January 15, 1958):

$$\frac{\text{Name-of-the-Father}}{\text{Desire of the Mother}} \cdot \frac{\text{Desire of the Mother}}{\text{Signified to the Subject}} \longrightarrow \text{Name-of-the-Father}\left(\frac{O}{\text{Phallus}}\right)$$

We find in this formula of the metaphor the general algorithm:

$$\frac{S2}{\cancel{S1}} \cdot \frac{\cancel{S1}}{s1} \longrightarrow S2\left(\frac{U}{s1}\right)$$

In the second term of the formula, the symbol U (unconscious) reminds us that S1 has been repressed via the substitution of S2, which is from now on the signifier associated with the signified (s1) of the desire of the mother, that is, the phallus. In the preceding formula we find the mark of this repression symbolized by O (Other), which indicates that

> [t]he presence of the signifier in the Other is, in effect, a presence usually closed to the subject, because it usually persists in a state of repression (it is *verdrängt*), and because from there it insists on representing itself in the signified by means of its repetition compulsion (*Wiederholungszwang*). [Lacan 1958b, p. 200, translation modified]

And in fact the repetition compulsion leads to the following conclusion: by "naming the Father" the child is really still naming the fundamental object of his desire. But now he names it metaphorically, since it has become unconscious for him. The symbol of language is therefore intended to express the permanence of the fundamental object of desire in a designation that takes place without the subject's knowledge. This amounts to saying, with Lacan, that language allows us to immortalize the expression of the primary object by socializing that expression in the symbolic register of intersubjective communication. This also sheds light on what is essentially at stake in the Oedipus complex: the metaphor of the Name-of-the-Father bears witness to the actualization of *castration*, which operates on the only level on which it is intelligible, as *symbolic castration*. This is why the phallus appears, at the end of the oedipal process, as the symbolic loss of an imaginary object.

THE METONYMY OF DESIRE

By means of primal repression and the paternal metaphor, the mediation of language is imposed on desire. More precisely, it is the paternal signifier that inaugurates the *alienation of desire in language*. In becoming speech, desire becomes a mere reflection of itself. When the child represses the *desire to be* in favor of the *desire to have*, he must from then on engage his desire in the realm of objects that are substitutes for the object he has lost. To accomplish this, desire must become speech in the form of a *demand*. But in becoming demand, desire gets more and more lost in the signifying chain of discourse. Indeed, we can say that desire moves from object to object, always referring to an indefinite series of substitutes and at the same time to a indefinite series of signifiers that symbolize these substitute objects. It therefore persists in designating, unbeknownst to him, the subject's original desire.

Desire remains forever unsatisfied because it had to become language. And so it is continually reborn, since it is always fundamentally elsewhere, not in its object of the moment or in the signifier that might symbolize that object. In other words, *the path of desire is metonymic*. The metaphor of the Name-of-the-Father requires the child to take a part (the substitute object) for the whole (the lost object). In the same way as "a sail on the horizon" designates the whole (the ship) by the part (the sail), desire persists in designating the desire for the whole (the lost object) by the expression of desire for the part (substitute objects).

In conclusion, the paternal metaphor marks the beginning of a radically structuring phase in the psychic development of the child. In addition to inaugurating his access to the symbolic dimension by freeing him from his imaginary subjection to his mother, it gives him the status of *desiring subject*. The benefit of this acquisition is attained, however, only at the price of a new alienation. For as soon as the "speakingbeing" [*le parlêtre*] becomes a desiring subject, his desire is taken captive by language and its original nature is lost. From here on it can be represented only by substitute signifiers that transform the object of desire into a *metonymic object*.

Thus, for Lacan, the metaphor of the Name-of-the-Father is truly a structural crossroads, with important consequences. Its implications are numerous. When it fails, psychotic processes develop; when it succeeds, it alienates the desire of the subject in the dimension of language by establishing a subjective division (*Spaltung*) that irreversibly separates him from a part of himself as the unconscious comes into being. These consequences are what we have to look at now.

14

The Foreclosure of the
Name-of-the-Father:
An Approach to Psychotic Processes

The paternal metaphor has a structuring function in that it founds the psychic subject as such. By the same token, if something blocks the process of primal repression, the paternal metaphor does not occur. Basing himself on the work of Freud, Lacan developed quite original ideas on this subject:

> Let us now try to conceive of a circumstance of the subjective position in which the appeal to the Name-of-the-Father is answered, not by the absence of the real father, for this absence is more than compatible with the presence of the signifier, but by the *inadequacy of the signifier itself.* . . .
>
> Let us extract from several of Freud's texts a term that is sufficiently articulated in them to render them unjustifiable if this term does not designate in them a function of the unconscious that is distinct from the repressed. Let us take as demonstrated the essence of my seminar on the psychoses [1955–1956], namely that this term refers to the most necessary implication of his thought when it comes to grips with the phenomenon of psychosis: this term is *Verwerfung.* [Lacan 1958b, p. 200, translation modified]

Verwerfung, translated as *foreclosure*, seems to be the very mechanism that can cause primal repression to fail. This thesis constitutes the essence of Lacan's original contribution to the Freudian tradition of reflections on the metapsychological distinction between the neuroses and the psychoses.

Since the second half of the nineteenth century, psychiatric thinking has been continually stimulated by the need to formulate this distinction in a way that is theoretically relevant and clinically operative. One major line of thought has focused on examining the hypothesis that psychosis is psychogenic. In this respect Freud's work created a radical upheaval, one that we might call doubly subversive—first because Freud seemed to have deliberately broken away from the organogenic hypotheses of the time, and then because, by putting the notion of psychosis to the test of analytic theory, Freud was able to exhibit the data supporting a psychic etiology that was, to say the least, original. And the uniqueness of his conception is quite bold indeed. He approaches the special features of the psychotic process in a body of theoretical propositions originally intended to explain the etiology of the neuroses. And he also attempts to base his argument on structural considerations and not on mere qualitative and differential ones.

As innovative it was, the Freudian psychoanalytic conception of psychosis remains unsatisfactory in that it does not succeed in giving a detailed account of the etiology of the psychotic process. In particular, the theoretical arguments that Freud advanced do not enable us to work out a sufficiently operational criterion for the structural differentiation between the neuroses and the psychoses. The Freudian account of psychosis is somehow overdetermined by the psychiatric conceptions of his time. The clearest indications of this overdetermination probably lie in Freud's conception of the subject's relation to reality in the psychoses.

We know that Freud (1924a,b) first defined the nature of the psychotic process in terms of "loss of reality" and of its correlative effect on the subject, the need to reconstruct in the form of delusions the reality from which he had been cut off. Though he approached these two aspects of the psychotic process from a resolutely psychoanalytic point of view, Freud nevertheless remained the captive of a contemporary psychiatric stereotype that led him to see the loss of reality and the delusional construction as being in a relationship of cause to effect. As a result, given the quasi-logical reciprocity between these two signs of the psychotic presentation, one could almost posit delusional manifestations as the pathognomonic criterion for psychosis.

Apart from the fact that this semiological point is altogether problematic, toward the end of his career Freud developed a more nuanced distinction between neurosis and psychosis as far as the question of loss of reality is concerned. He described the neurotic subject as *fleeing* reality while the psychotic subject *disavows* it. Deeper reflection on the concept of *Ichspaltung* ("splitting of the ego") led him to this revision (Freud 1938a,b). Loss of reality now appears as only a partial break, since only a part of the ego is cut off from reality in the psychoses. Moreover, the splitting of the ego may be present not only in the psychoses but also in the neuroses and perversions, as the problematics of fetishism had already led him to think (Freud 1927). In short, the splitting of the ego cannot constitute an operative metapsychological criterion for differentiating the neuroses from the psychoses any more than can the loss of reality.

Lacan turns the Freudian notion of psychic splitting to good account with regard to the matter we have been considering, the consequences of the paternal metaphor. It is primarily one of these consequences that leads him to posit foreclosure as an operative metapsychological criterion for distinguishing psychotic processes. First, the notion of foreclosure, according to Lacan, enables us to understand why certain mechanisms characteristic of neurosis—repression in particular—do not explain the emergence of the psychotic process; second, we can see how the mechanism of foreclosure specifies the psychotic process when it applies to one signifier in particular, the Name-of-the-Father. It is on this latter point that Lacan has made his most explicit contribution to Freudian thought. If the Name-of-the-Father is foreclosed in the place of the Other, the paternal metaphor fails and this, for Lacan, constitutes "the defect that gives psychosis its essential condition and the structure that separates it from neurosis" (Lacan 1955–1956, p. 215).

In other words, the foreclosure of the Name-of-the-Father, which blocks the occurrence of primal repression, simultaneously leads to the failure of the paternal metaphor and seriously compromises, even prohibits, the child's access to the symbolic order. Structural advancement in the register of desire is suspended, and the child remains stuck in an archaic organization, captive of the imaginary dual relationship with the mother.

An excellent illustration of the effects of this foreclosure of the Name-of-the-Father is to be found in one of the clinical studies presented by Patris (1981). In his case report on little Anne, Patris clearly describes two of the clinical elements commonly found in cases where the paternal function has failed. First, there is foreclosure of the Name-of-the-Father when *this signifier is denied in the mother's discourse*. Second, there is the *circulation of the phallus in the maternal genealogy;* this excludes the symbolic father and thus also any possibility of symbolizing the law of the father by establishing symbolic castration. In these two clinical elements we find one of the lines of force of Lacan's (1955–1956) thought on signifying causality in the emergence of psychotic processes.

> What I do wish to insist on is that we should concern our- selves not only with the way in which the mother accom- modates herself to the person of the father, but also with the importance she accords to his speech, to—let us say the word—his authority, that is, *to the place that she reserves for the Name-of-the-Father in the promulgation of the law.* [p. 218, emphasis added, translation modified]

Let us leave, for the time being, the Lacanian approach to the psychoses. We shall return to this subject later, after an ex- amination of another fundamental consequence of the paternal metaphor: *the splitting of the subject (Spaltung)* and the effect of this splitting on the organization of delusional discourse (see Chapter 22).

15

The Division of the Subject and the Advent of the Unconscious through the Signifying Order

The metaphor of the Name-of-the-Father is a foundational process in psychic development for more than one reason. Not only does it permit the child's emergence as a subject by giving him access to the symbolic order (and to the practice of the mother tongue), but it also institutes an irreversible psychic division (*Spaltung*) in that subject. The mechanism of the paternal metaphor is based entirely on an effect of a signifier, namely signifying substitution. Strictly speaking, therefore, it is the order of signifiers that establishes the subject in his divided structure. This is another way of saying that *the subject is divided by the very order of language*. Since the paternal metaphor is also grounded in primal repression, that is, in the advent of the unconscious, it follows that the unconscious, as such, is likewise subject to the signifying order. This metapsychological organization, which is without a doubt the most crucial argument in favor of the thesis of the unconscious structured like a language, needs to be examined in detail with regard to its constituting principles and its implications.

The very notion of *Spaltung* calls for several preliminary terminological remarks. As Laplanche and Pontalis (1973) point out, the concept of psychic division had already been implicitly formulated in several studies on psychopathology at the end of the nineteenth century, especially in works on hypnosis and hysteria. For it is in the sense of a psychic division of the subject that we must understand—to cite only two examples—terms such as *double consciousness* or *psychic dissociation* as they appear in Breuer's and Freud's (1893–1895) *Studies on Hysteria*. The notion of psychic division is elaborated by Janet, but above all by Breuer and Freud. Later we find it expressed under different names: *splitting of consciousness, splitting of the content of consciousness, psychic splitting*. It is these terms that give substance to the Freudian notion of the unconscious. As early as 1893 Freud indisputably established that in hysteria the conscious subject is cut off from a part of his representations. The unconscious therefore appears as an autonomous region, separated from the field of consciousness by the effects of repression. In this sense we can already consider such a psychic division to be a division of the subject.

In Freud's work psychic division also finds suitable expression in the term *Ichspaltung*, or *splitting of the ego*. Freud (1927, 1938a,b) gradually delineated this notion, distinguishing splitting of the ego from psychic division proper. As Laplanche and Pontalis (1973) point out, the splitting of the ego is primarily an *intrasystemic splitting*, an internal splitting within that agency. On the other hand, the psychic division described by Freud and Breuer (1893–1895) in *Studies on Hysteria*, is, from the outset, *intersystemic*. Referring briefly to the second topography, one could speak of a division between the ego and the id.

Thus, for Freud, the notion of *Spaltung* appears to be relatively polyvalent. It reminds us that the psychic apparatus is divided into agencies, and it also indicates that a psychic agency is divided within itself. Finally, on a more general level, it specifies that the subject may be cut off from a part of his psychic contents through the action of repression.

One last preliminary remark on the signification of the term *Spaltung* as it appears in the field of psychiatry with the work of Bleuler. Bleuler's (1911) *Spaltung* can in no way be confused with that of Freud. For Bleuler, the term has a very particular meaning that refers to a primary clinical factor in the schizophrenias. As such, *Spaltung* belongs to a group of semiological considerations and to a principle of the organization of psychic functioning that are quite foreign to the metapsychological perspectives of psychoanalysis. Bleuler's *Spaltung* is known as "dissociation" nowadays and in contemporary psychiatry refers exclusively to the schizophrenic syndromes.

For Lacan, *Spaltung* is unequivocally the most foundational feature defining subjectivity, since it is the means through which the subject comes into being and, as he does so, takes on a given psychic structure. It is not, therefore, an intrasystemic splitting. Nor is it intersystemic. For Lacan, *Spaltung* is that which *establishes* the psychic apparatus as being plurisystemic. In this sense it may be considered as the inaugural division of the subject that proceeds from the subject's own subjection to a third order, the Symbolic. More precisely, this symbolic order mediates the subject's relation to the Real by knotting together the Real and the Imaginary orders for him. This binding occurs during the establishment of the paternal metaphor. At the end of this process a symbol of language (the Name-of-the-Father signifier, or S2) comes to designate metaphorically the primordial object of desire that has become unconscious (signifier of the mother's desire, the phallic signifier S1).

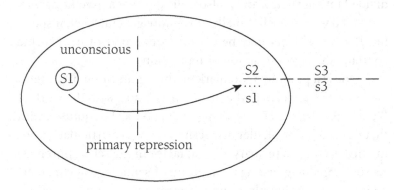

If the child thus continues, *without knowing it,* to name the object of his desire by using the Name-of-the-Father as signifier, we can come to only one conclusion: the child no longer knows what he is saying in what he utters. Language therefore appears as that subjective activity in which *we say something completely different from what we believe we are saying when we speak.* This "something completely different" is installed as the unconscious that escapes the speaking subject because he is constitutively separated from it.

By virtue of this subjective division brought about by the signifying order, language appears as that which is *the condition of* the unconscious by causing it to come into being and by maintaining it as a locus of selection. Lacan insists upon this point: "Language is the condition for the unconscious. . . . The unconscious is the logical implication of language: in effect, no unconscious without language" (Lemaire 1977, p. xiii).

To say that the subject is divided is, according to Lacan, to posit that there is no subject other than the speaking being, the *parlêtre.* It is also to recognize that the causing of the subject is based on the promoting of the unconscious. In other words, the signifying order causes the subject by structuring him in a process of division that founds the unconscious.

These fundamental theses of Lacan's theoretical work broke radically with contemporary psychoanalytic thought. An example of this is the dispute that arose during the famous Bonneval conference on the unconscious organized by Ey in 1960. On this occasion Jean Laplanche (Laplanche and Leclaire 1966) came to diametrically opposite conclusions by endorsing the thesis that the unconscious is the condition of language. This led to an explanatory intervention on Lacan's part (Lacan 1960a).

Through this structural division of the subject, *primal repression* plays an essential role in the advent of the unconscious. We have seen that primal repression bears selectively on the signifier of the mother's desire (the phallic signifier). It is, of course, a didactic simplification to speak of *the* phallic signifier. In fact, there are probably several different signifiers that can serve as phallic signifiers, all of them able to designate something of the order of the mother's desire. Let us call them *primordial signifiers*. They are signifiers that lend themselves to metaphoric substitution, as a result of which they constitute an unconscious nucleus, the *primally repressed*.

This primal repression of primordial signifiers must be set in the context of Freud's (1915c) theory of repression. Here Freud describes repression as a mechanism organized in three phases: primal repression; repression proper or repression after the event; and the return of the repressed in formations of the unconscious. Repression proper is induced by primal repression, which refers to the nucleus of strongly cathected basic representations—in other words, to the primordial signifiers connected with the mother's desire. Because of this cathexis the original unconscious nucleus is powerfully attractive. This is why

Freud describes primal repression as a process of anticathexis, saying that it "represents the permanent expenditure [of energy] of primal repression, and . . . also guarantees the permanence of that repression. Anticathexis is the sole mechanism of primal repression" (Freud 1915b, p. 181).

This being the case, we can put forward the argument that it is because the paternal signifier is the object of a powerful anticathexis that the signifier of the mother's desire can be repressed and maintained in the unconscious. This primally repressed content is therefore able to exert a very strong attraction upon other possible contents (signifiers)—all the more so with the addition of repelling forces coming from the superior agencies, the ego and the superego. Secondary repression, or repression proper, is established on the basis of this double process. It thereby in a way perpetuates the division of the subject founded by the paternal metaphor. Secondary repression also establishes the unconscious as a locus of signifiers organized discursively, that is, as a signifying organization *analogous* to that of a language that the subject no longer has at his disposal. For this reason Lacan states that *the unconscious is the discourse of the Other* (the discourse of the subject's "other" that, because of the *Spaltung*, escapes him).

The advent of this signifying organization in the locus of the unconscious can be expressed metaphorically by the diagram on page 133.

This diagram illustrates the progressive constitution of the unconscious signifying chain organized by the occurrence of successive "metaphoric repressions." As such, this chain of unconscious signifiers is subject to the primary process. The repressed signifiers, therefore, may always reappear for the subject through metaphoric and/or metonymic signifying substitutions. An example of this is the slip of the tongue that

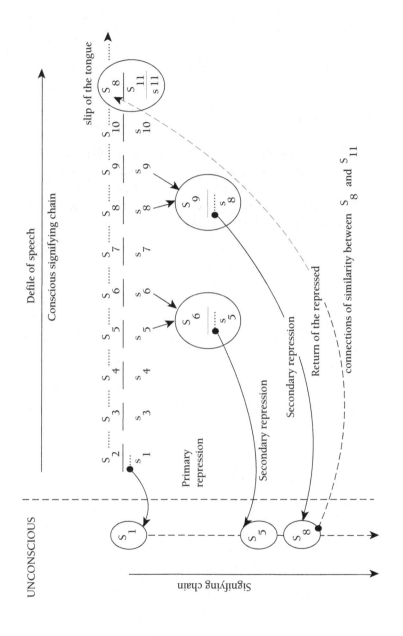

bursts into the conscious spoken chain by means of a substitution such as:

$$\frac{\dfrac{S8}{S11}}{s11}$$

And, as Lacan notes,

> a minimal combination from the battery of signifiers is all that is needed to set up in the signifying chain a duplicity that conceals its reduplication of the subject, and it is in this doubling of the subject in speech that the unconscious as such can articulate itself. [Lacan 1959, p. 711]

16

The Splitting of the Subject: Alienation in Language

The division of the subject produced by the signifying order establishes another fundamental property of subjectivity, the alienation of the subject in and by language as a result of the type of relation he maintains to the symbolic order. It is in this relation that the subject reveals his radically inessential nature insofar as he fades in some way as subject into the signifying chain.

The basic property of linguistic utterance is to evoke a reality by means of a symbolic substitute that inevitably causes a split between experienced reality and that which comes to signify it. In other words, the symbolic substitute that signifies this reality is not the reality itself but its representative. This is the sense of Lacan's aphorism, "The thing must be lost in order to be represented." Language therefore has the singular property of representing the presence of a reality to the advantage of the absence of this reality as such. As Lacan (1953) puts it, "Through the word, which is already a presence made of absence, absence itself comes to be named" (p. 65, translation modified).

Since this is so, the relation of the subject to his own discourse is based on the same effect of division. This means that the subject figures in his own discourse only at the price of this division; he disappears as subject and finds himself, in what he says, represented only in the form of a symbol. This is precisely the process that Miller (1966) calls the "suture," that which "names the relation of the subject to the chain of his discourse"; the subject "figures [in his discourse] as the missing element, under the aspect of a stand-in. For, while he is missing in it, he is not purely and simply absent" (p. 39). And we know that it is the purpose of certain privileged symbols to carry out this mission: the pronouns "I/me," "you," "he," "we," and so on. These are, etymologically, the pronouns that stand "in place of the name" and thereby ensure the symbolic representation of the subject in his discourse.

The relation of the subject to his own discourse is therefore based on a unique effect: the subject can be *made present* in it only if *he is absent from it in his essence.* This relation once again shows the structural division of the subject, and at the same time it reveals how the subject, having acquired language, immediately loses himself in that very language that caused him. *The subject is not the cause of language but is caused by it.* This means that the subject who comes into being through language is inserted into it only in the form of an effect: no sooner is the subject brought into existence by language than he is eclipsed in the authenticity of his being. Lacan refers to this eclipse as the *fading of the subject.* The subject can perceive himself through his language only as a representation, a mask, that alienates him by concealing him from himself. This alienation of the subject in his own discourse is what is meant by the *splitting of the subject.*

Language is a system of signs in opposition, such that one signifier in a signifying chain acquires meaning only through its relation to all the others. This property, which Saussure (1966) calls the *value of the sign*, is coextensive with the Lacanian notion of the *anchoring point* (see Chapter 5).

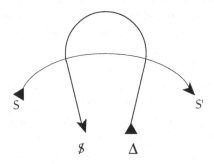

The anchoring point is a metaphor for that property of language by virtue of which a signifier in a spoken chain acquires meaning only retroactively. The last signifier of the chain is what gives meaning, after the fact, to the preceding ones. This is indicated by the reversed direction of the anchoring vector: $\overrightarrow{\Delta \text{\$}}$.

The process of the paternal metaphor, then, concludes with the point that, since it is through the signifying order that the subject arises, he is always merely represented in the language that caused him. The foremost consequence of this, one that inserts the subject into the order of his discourse, is that *a signifier is that which represents a subject for another signifier*. This consequence is inevitably brought about by the intrinsic structure of the language system. If the subject figures in discourse only as a representative, and if, moreover, it is a signifier that gives him the status of subject in discourse, then this can only be in relation to another signifier. This is why the subject is an effect of the signifier, and only an effect. In no way can he be the cause of the signifier. The Lacanian notion of the *barred Subject* (**\$**) is based on this idea. The subject comes into being exclusively as a subject barred by the signifying order, that is, barred to himself:

> The register of the signifier is established on the basis of the fact that one signifier represents a subject for another signifier. This is the structure, dream, slip of the tongue, joke, of all the formations of the unconscious. It is also the one that explains the original division of the subject.
>
> The signifier coming from the place of the Other (not yet located) makes the subject of the being who does not yet have speech emerge there, but at the price of immobilizing him. What was there that was ready to speak . . . disappears and is no longer anything but a signifier. [Lacan 1960a, p. 840]

Furthermore,

> The effect of language is the cause introduced into the subject. By virtue of this effect, he is not the cause of himself: he bears within himself the worm of the cause that splits him. For his cause is the signifier, without which there would be no subject in the real. But this subject is what this signifier represents, and it can never represent anything except for another signifier, to which, from that point on, the listening subject is reduced.
>
> So we don't speak to the subject. *That*[1] speaks of him, and it is there that he apprehends himself—and all the more necessarily so since, before he disappears as a subject beneath

---

1. Translator's note: *Le ça,* literally, "the that," is the French translation of Freud's *das Es,* "the It," which is commonly rendered into English as "the id." The use in English of this Latin word for "it" conveys neither the familiarity of the everyday German or French words "it" or "that," nor (paradoxically) the otherness of this third-person agency within the self.

the signifier that he becomes because of the sole fact that *that* addresses him, he was absolutely nothing. But this nothing depends on his advent, which is now brought about by the appeal made in the Other to the second signifier. [Lacan 1960a, p. 835]

Let us further clarify the meaning and scope of this fundamental Lacanian thesis that a signifier is what represents a subject for another signifier. The principle of the paternal metaphor is the primary illustration of this statement. In the metaphor of the Name-of-the-Father, it is the advent of S2, replacing S1, that brings forth the speaking subject; S2 is therefore the signifier that represents the subject in relation to another signifier, S1. The same process is repeated progressively as the signifying chain constitutes itself (see Chapter 15), since the spoken chain is structured in such a way that the meaning of one sign depends on the meaning of all the other signs. However, the meaning of the sign is somehow also dependent upon an act of symbolization that is the construction of the sign itself by association of a signifier to a signified. This sign comes about, therefore, only because a subject participates in its elaboration. In this sense, we can define the meaning of the sign as that which *represents* the intervention of a subject. Since the meaning of the sign depends on the meaning of the other signs, it therefore actualizes the intervention of a subject in relation to the meaning of another sign. So we are justified in putting aside both the meaning and the sign as such by virtue of the primacy of the signifier over the signified. If we retain the signifier alone, it is thus apparent that a signifier is in fact that which represents a subject for another signifier.

Here a point needs to be clarified. What about the signified in this relation to the signifier? To answer this, we must go back to our starting point, that is, to primal repression. Let us take another look at the diagram of the foundational moment of the paternal metaphor and the establishment of the spoken chain, and complete it in the following manner (see page 141).

As soon as the paternal metaphor is constituted, the child who is acquiring language no longer knows what he is saying (the repressed S1) on the level of what he is uttering (S2). In the "defile of speech" the spoken chain organizes itself as a discrete succession of signs, or signifiers associated with signifieds. Certain circumstances can lead to secondary repressions occurring in the form of metaphoric processes. As a result of these processes, certain other signifiers then become unconscious (S5 and S8 in the diagram). This does not mean that $\frac{S5}{s5}$ and $\frac{S8}{s8}$ have disappeared from the spoken chain. They remain present in it as available constructions governed by the code of language. In his lexicon the subject can still use these signs with their precise meanings, which does not rule out their having been combined, outside his awareness, in metaphoric mechanisms. In other words, the difference between repressed signifiers (S5 and S8) and these same signifiers in speech is their mode of inscription in the unconscious chain and in the spoken chain. Thus it is the signifying function that varies, beyond the signifier proper.

The repressed signifiers make their comeback into the life of the subject in the form, for example, of subversions of the spoken chain such as slips of the tongue ($\frac{\frac{S8}{S11}}{s11}$ in the diagram).

This may also occur in a metaphoric condensation in a dream.

Perhaps the most telling illustration here is the phobia and the establishment of the phobic signifier. Let us take as an example a clinical vignette of a leather phobia in a young woman. This phobia, which was first attached to leather goods, was later extended to leather garments and furniture. Like most phobias,

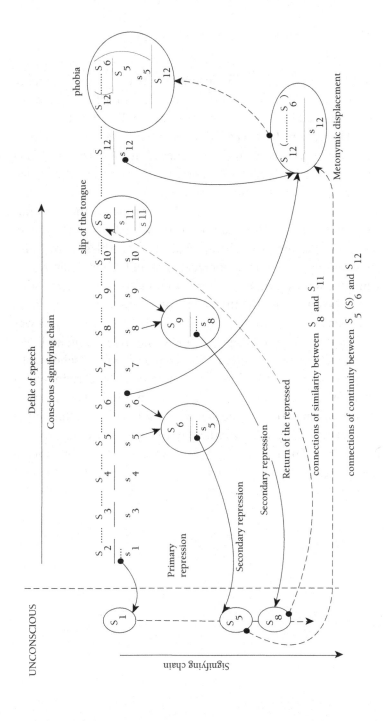

it was triggered one day for no apparent reason. Analysis gradually revealed material that made it possible to define the significant elements in the elaboration of the phobic object.

The patient first recalled an event that had taken place at about the same time as the appearance of the phobia: her mother gave her a leather handbag for her fifteenth birthday. Much later, she remembered her mother threatening her in a context she associated with a traumatic scene. During a visit to the zoo when she was 6 years old she had been throwing food to the crocodiles. She was terrified when one of the crocodiles snapped his jaws sharply, with a violent cracking sound. Shortly thereafter, while she was masturbating during a children's game, her mother had intervened with the threat, "If you continue with your filth, I'll have your hand cut off in the crocodile's mouth!" In this way the *crocodile* became a signifier for *sexual repression*, and, at a deeper level, for *castration*. A few years later, in school, she learned that crocodile skin was used to produce certain *leather goods*. At this point all the favorable conditions were in place for the organization of the signifying substitutions that led to the onset of the phobia on the day that her mother gave her a leather bag. The mother's gift, as it were, catalyzed the unconscious signifying associations that reactivated the threat of castration and the maternal disapproval of her sexual activity:

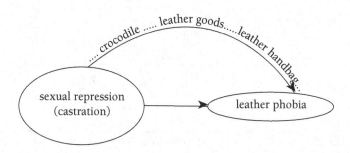

The leather phobia appears as the combined result of a metaphoric repression and an unconscious metonymic displacement. Referring to the schema on page 141, let us posit the following elements:

$$\frac{S5}{s5} \qquad \text{sexual repression}$$
$$\qquad\qquad \text{(castration)}$$

$$\frac{S6}{s6} \qquad \text{crocodile}$$

$$\frac{S12}{s12} \qquad \text{leather}$$

We can therefore account for the way in which the phobia was constructed by the following series of unconscious processes:

The first signifier, S5, became unconscious as a result of a metaphoric repression:

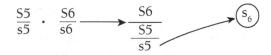

During this process, a new signifier, S6 (crocodile), replaces signifier S5 (sexual repression/castration), which becomes unconscious. In other words, S6 continues to function on the conscious level as the ordinary signifier for "crocodile," but at the same time, on the unconscious level, it is a signifier that from now on metaphorizes the "sexual repression/castration" whose specific signifier has been repressed. S6 thus becomes an unconscious "metaphoric crocodile."

A second signifying process subsequently takes place by means of an unconscious metonymic displacement. When the little girl learns that crocodile skin is used to produce leather objects, the signifier "leather" (S12) becomes itself a metonymic signifier of the "crocodile" S6 :

$$\frac{S6}{s6} \quad \frac{S12}{s12} \longrightarrow \frac{S12 (..... S6)}{s12} \longrightarrow \left(s_6\right)$$

An unfortunate act on the mother's part suffices to trigger the phobia: the gift of the leather handbag. This act crystallizes a final signifying substitution resulting in the actual leather phobia, which is triggered when the signifier S6 (crocodile), as seen in the preceding metonymic construction, suddenly starts to function as what it is unconsciously, that is, the "metaphoric crocodile," so that the signifier "leather" (S12) becomes metonymically linked to the repressed signifier of sexual repression, S5. The leather phobia can therefore be diagrammed as the following signifying substitution:

$$\text{leather phobia} \Longleftrightarrow \frac{S12 \left(........ \dfrac{S6}{\frac{S5}{s5}}\right)}{s12} \nearrow \left(s_6\right)$$

The result of these successive signifying substitutions makes it clear that, at one and the same time, the signifier "leather" signifies something entirely different from the idea of leather. This is why this woman knows what leather is, but at the same time *does not know* why she is terrified by it. And she cannot know, because, beyond the ordinary reference that S12 continues to have for her, it is also metaphorically and metonymically linked, without her knowledge, to the unconscious signifier S5.

In conclusion, it is clear that the destiny of the signified is secondary with regard to the signifier. From the point of view of the unconscious, only substitutions of signifiers are decisive. In this sense the relation of the subject to the chain of his own discourse is above all a relation of alienation from and by the signifier. Although the signifieds continue to play their own role, the splitting of the subject is, *par excellence*, what defines the alienation of the speakingbeing [*parlêtre*] from the chain of signifiers. Additional proof of this, as we shall see, is the radical subjection of the truth of the subject's desire to the order of discourse.

17

Subject of the Unconscious–Subject of the Enunciation—Subject of the Utterance

From the Lacanian perspective, the division of the subject implies the definition of a part of our subjectivity as subject of the unconscious or subject of desire. The subject's relation to his discourse under the influence of the *Spaltung* imposes this conclusion. Lacan (1960a) expresses it concisely: "So we don't speak to the subject. *That* speaks of him, and it is there that he apprehends himself" (p. 835).

All the metapsychological consequences of the fact that the subject is divided by the signifying order are implicitly brought together in these two formulas. The "*that* speaks" refers to the subject in his being, in the authenticity and the truth of his desire. Obviously, the subject can never speak this truth himself, since he is always only represented in his own discourse. He can only make it speak. We realize that, from the time of the onset of the paternal metaphor, it is S2 that makes S1 speak, because the subject's desire (S1) can make itself understood only in the form of a substitute signifier (S2). The subject in the truth of his desire is therefore concealed from himself by the dimension of language. Conversely, *that* speaks of the subject's desire in his discourse unbeknownst to him. In this sense, then, desire is strictly coextensive with the register of the unconscious. *The subject in the truth of his desire can therefore be posited as the subject of the unconscious.* The "*that* speaks of him," designating this subject of the unconscious, is what we are inexorably cut off from, so that we are merely represented in language. Correlatively, the speaking subject constantly articulates something of his desire in the "defile of speech." I propose the following illustration to schematize this influence of the subject of the unconscious, of the subject of desire, in signifying articulation:

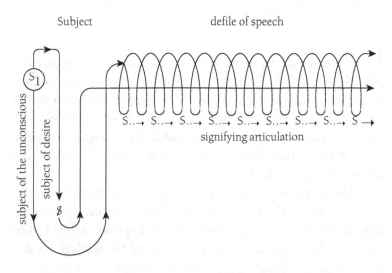

However, the language that establishes the subject as $\$$ is an enterprise of speech and as such must be brought into relation with the usual structure of discourse. Now the articulation of a discourse has two aspects: the *utterance* [*énoncé*] and the act of *enunciation* [*énonciation*] of this utterance. This classic distinction in linguistics is fundamental to Lacan's view of the relationship of the speaking subject to the unconscious and to desire.

Before examining Lacan's use of the distinction between utterance and enunciation to get the heart of the unconscious and its subject, let us review the meanings and implications of this distinction in the field of linguistics. What, in linguistics, is an utterance? First, it is a finite series of words brought forth by a speaker. The closure of an utterance is generally ensured by a silence produced by the speaking subject to punctuate his articulation. Moreover, each type of discourse is characterized by a succession of qualitatively different utterances. The contrast between enunciation and utterance is based on the same type of distinction as can be made between the *process of manufacturing* and the *manufactured object*. If enunciation is, in effect, an individual language act, then the utterance must be considered to be the result of an act of creation on the part of a speaking subject.

For this reason, enunciation raises a number of linguistic problems, beginning with the very fact that it is a language act, that is, an intentional initiative on the part of the speaker. There are numerous factors and acts contributing to the production of an utterance. Certain schools of linguistics have systematically explored this property of the speech act; two of the principal figures are J. L. Austin (1962) of the Oxford school of linguistics and John R. Searle (1969), who has dealt extensively with the problematics of the enunciation. Austin, in particular, has attempted to identify what happens when we produce an enunciation. He at first played down the importance of certain utterances commonly privileged in philosophy, namely affirmative statements. For in fact, certain statements can be declared true or false from the point of view of the act of enunciation. Thus Austin differentiated between authentic statements resulting from *constative utterances* and those that *do* something without being declared true or false, *performative utterances*. These latter acts of enunciation allow us to do things by the very use of speech. It is in this sense that Austin was led to the conclusion that every utterance is above all a speech act, and, as such, aims to accomplish something.

In a later stage of his research, Austin attempted to isolate the aspect of this act of enunciation that defines it as an act of speech; he calls this aspect the illocutionary force of speech. In other words, what we are dealing with here is an aspect of speech that can accomplish something insofar as it is part of an act. Austin cites the following example of a performative utterance. To the traditional question, "Do you take X to be your lawful wedded wife/husband?," the "I do" that generally comes in response is a performative "I do."

> I began by drawing your attention, by way of example, to a few simple utterances of the kind known as performatories or performatives. These have on the face of them the look— or at least the grammatical make-up—of 'statements'; but nevertheless they are seen, when more closely inspected, to be, quite plainly, *not* utterances which could be 'true' or 'false'. Yet to be 'true' or 'false' is traditionally the characteristic mark of a statement. One of our examples was, for instance, the utterance 'I do' (take this woman to be my lawful wedded wife), as uttered in the course of a marriage ceremony. Here we should say that in saying these words we are *doing* something—namely, marrying, rather than *reporting* something, namely *that* we are marrying. [Austin 1962, p. 12]

Austin's distinction here is certainly not a minor one, in that it demonstrates that *the enunciation is not strictly uniform with the production of the utterance*. Because of this, enunciation can be defined, in linguistics, by a certain number of parameters. The most important of these is the portrayal of the subject in his utterance; it refers to the nature of the representative standing for the subject in his utterance, namely the *subject of the utterance*. This parameter will always present the subject of the utterance in a particular way, according to whether he is explicitly present in it, or on the contrary relatively absent.

Most often it is with "I" that the subject actualizes himself in his own utterances. But the subject of the utterance may also be adequately represented by "one," "you," "we," and so on. These pronouns are a way for the subject to show a certain subjective neutrality with regard to what he is saying, as is the rule, for example in didactic discourse. In this type of discourse, characterized by gnomic utterances, the subject articulates general or universal propositions, such as "The earth revolves around the sun" or "Men are said to be mortal."

These utterances do indeed create a distance between the subject of the utterance and the enunciation. On the other hand, this distance seems to diminish when the subject says something about himself: "I am going to the movies." But the "I" in this sort of utterance is nonetheless a representative of the subject in discourse—more precisely, a representative called forth by the subject in the very act of his enunciation. The subject of the utterance, in the strict sense of the term, must therefore be distinguished from the directly subjective participation that calls him forth as subject in a discourse. This subjective participation actualizing a representative as subject of the utterance in a discourse may be called the *subject of the enunciation*. It is the speaker considered as a subjective entity and as the locus and agent of the production of utterances.

Thus there is, in a sense, a contrast between the subject of the utterance and the subject of the enunciation, which reinforces the opposition established within the subject by his division.

The distinction between the subject of the utterance and
the subject of the enunciation is directly related to the fundamental opposition that Lacan specifies between the "said" and
the "saying," and to its consequence regarding *the truth of the
subject that can only ever be half-said*. Here we may refer to an
observation of Lacan's:

> "That doesn't go without saying"—we see that that is the case
> with many things, even with most of them, including the
> Freudian thing as I defined it as being the said [*le dit*] of the
> truth. . . . This is how the said doesn't go without saying. But
> if the said always presents itself as the truth, even if it never
> goes beyond a half-said [*un mi-dit*], the saying [*le dire*] is
> coupled with it only to ex-sist [*ex-sister*] there, that is, not
> to be of the spoken-dimension [*la dit-mension*] of the truth.
> [Lacan 1972, p. 8][1]

Since the subject comes into being through language, it is
therefore through the act of signifying articulation, that is,
through enunciation, that he does so. But, as we have seen, this
subject has no sooner come into being through language than
he is lost there in the truth of his being and is merely represented.
At the same time, the truth of the subject comes into being the
same way the subject does, namely in the articulation of language, *in its enunciation*. The subject of the unconscious, therefore, *the subject of desire, is to be found on the level of the subject of
the enunciation*. "In order to be situated in the locus of the Other,
the presence of the unconscious is to be sought in any discourse
in its enunciation" (Lacan 1960a, p. 834). The unconscious
therefore reveals itself in the *saying*, whereas in the *said* the truth
of the subject is lost, appearing only under the mask of the sub-

---

1. Translator's note: On *ex-sister* see Chapter 18.

ject of the utterance, where, in order to make itself heard, all it can do is half-say itself.

These oppositions, "utterance/enunciation" and "the said/ the saying," which actualize the divided structure of the subject, have logical consequences for psychoanalytic practice. This is especially so with regard to the problem of evenly suspended attention and the ambiguities it entails. The subjective contrast between the subject of the utterance and the subject of the enunciation, emphasized in Lacan's theory of the unconscious, represents an original approach to this problem.

In their article "Attention (Evenly) Suspended or Poised," Laplanche and Pontalis (1973) describe in detail the various difficulties posed by this particular subjective attitude of the analyst in clinical practice. The technical rule involves suspending, as completely as possible, the usual motivations that arouse and underlie attention in the form of inclinations, judgments, and other personal opinions. Suspended attention, according to Freud, favors the analyst's own unconscious activity in that it keeps him from granting, *a priori*, special importance to any of the diverse elements of the patient's discourse. Freud (1912) developed this thesis explicitly in "Recommendations to Physicians Practising Psycho-Analysis," where he specifies that it is through this subjective attitude that the analyst can take note of the multiplicity of elements in the patient's discourse, some of which will later prove to have unconscious connections to the desire of the subject.

Although Freud established evenly suspended attention as an attitude corresponding to that of the patient's free association, this rule raises certain fundamental problems, as Laplanche and Pontalis (1973) have observed. Let us first recall that the intuition underlying the principle of evenly suspended attention is based on the attempt to establish communication between the unconscious of the patient and that of the analyst. Freud (1912) explains it in the famous telephone metaphor:

> To put it in a formula: [the analyst] must turn his own unconscious like a receptive organ towards the transmitting unconscious of the patient. He must adjust himself to the patient as a telephone receiver is adjusted to the transmitting microphone. Just as the receiver converts back into sound-waves the electric oscillations in the telephone line which were set up by sound waves, so the doctor's unconscious is able, from the derivations of the unconscious which are communicated to him, to reconstruct that unconscious, which has determined the patient's free associations. [p. 115]

Such a procedure inevitably brings up a major question: How can evenly suspended attention free the analyst from the influence of his own unconscious motivations? Another problem arises from the previous one: On the basis of which specific factors should the analyst intervene if no one of them is, *a priori*, privileged in his listening?

Though the metapsychological concepts worked out by Lacan certainly do not allow us to resolve these various problems conclusively, they do at least offer an original perspective on technique. Because the unconscious appears in the discourse of the subject through the process of enunciation, the analyst's attention is suspended primarily on the level of the utterance and its subject. The acuteness of his listening, on the other hand, will be brought to bear on the register of the saying. If the analyst has to "plug" his unconscious into that of the patient, he must be especially receptive to the signifiers appearing in the act of saying, above and beyond the signifieds that are organized in what is said. The timeliness of his intervention is thus governed by the identification of these signifying effects, and the domain of the intervention therefore remains restricted to the signifying order.

Psychoanalytic intervention must also be separated from the problematics of insight to be encouraged in the patient, and from constructions elaborated on the basis of the material he brings in. In this perspective, the analyst's intervention, which also avoids the sterility of an explanatory interpretation, aims only at punctuating the patient's act of saying with a scansion that provides—right in the locus of enunciation—the signifying opening that makes itself heard in that place where it is destined to close up again with the closure of the utterance.

Here we must keep in mind that, as Lacan emphasized, "something that is said does not go without saying," an obvious fact that merely repeats the contrast between speech and language that he had confirmed from the "Rome Discourse" onward:

> We always come back, then, to our double reference to speech and to language. In order to free the subject's speech, we introduce him into the language of his desire, that is to say, into the *primary language* in which, beyond what he tells us of himself, he is already talking to us unknown to himself, and, in the first place, in the symbols of the symptom. [Lacan 1953b, p. 81]

The analytic intervention, therefore, has the status of an operation of language that occurs as a signifying cut in the order of what is said, so as to liberate the "primary language" of unconscious desire that is articulated in the act of saying.

18

The Alienation of the Subject in the Ego—Schema L— The Foreclosure of the Subject

The splitting of the subject of the enunciation from the subject of the utterance makes it clear that the two registers of subjectivity separated by the *Spaltung* can never coincide. The subject, present in his discourse only insofar as he is *represented* in it, is thereby committed to a project of semblance. Since he appears only in the form of a stand-in, his discourse is necessarily one of pretense with regard to the truth of his desire. In fact, the division of the subject is a breach open to every enticement, every lure. The lure comes about because the subject's utterances about himself perpetuate a hoax in which he is completely alienated within the imaginary register. In other words, the access to the symbolic order, which allows the subject to free himself from the imaginary dimension in which he was initially captured, ends up precipitating him even deeper into it.

The "I" of the utterance, as it were immobilized in the order of discourse, gradually obscures the subject of desire. This concealment establishes an *imaginary objectification of the subject*, who has no choice but to identify more and more with the different stand-ins who represent him in his discourse. He thus enters into a total misrecognition of who he is in terms of his desire. The numerous stand-ins among which the subject loses himself tend to be condensed into one imaginary representation that will become the only one that the subject, from then on, will be able to assume as his own, the only one through which he will be able to perceive himself.

The subject's imaginary objectification of himself is called the *ego*.[1] And to say that *the ego takes itself for the I* is, therefore, to emphasize the imaginary captivity to which the speakingbeing (*le parlêtre*) becomes more and more subjected. Since the ego is an imaginary construction by which the subject objectifies himself for himself through his stand-ins, the whole of subjectivity is thus undermined by a paradox.

The mirror stage is the inaugural phase of psychic development during which the child frees himself from his captivity in the dual relation to his mother. The outlines of subjectivity that are defined through the achievement of primal identity allow the child to begin his subjective movement toward access to the symbolic, where he will put an end to his imaginary, specular relation with the mother. Yet it is precisely through this access

---

1. Translator's note: The Latin pronoun *ego* is used in the *Standard Edition* to translate Freud's *das Ich*, "the I," which is rendered in French as *le moi*, "the me," in accordance with the simplicity and immediacy of the German original. (Cf. *le ça*, "the that," where the *Standard Edition* has the Latin "id.") *Moi* is in the objective case ("me" as opposed to "I"), which makes it especially appropriate for Lacan's usage as defined in this passage. Freud's *Ich*, like the Latin *ego*, is nominative, the grammatical case of the subject, but Lacan uses the nominative *le Je* in a different sense, for the subject's fading "I." In translating *le moi* as "the ego" I am following convention, but it is important to note that for Lacan "the ego" is not the same as "the subject."

to the symbolic that the subject's relapse into the imaginary occurs, culminating in the advent of the ego. A paradoxical economy such as this is best summed up in Lacan's (1960c) formula: "The drama of the subject in the word is that it is there that he puts his lack-of-being to the test" (p. 655). This lack-of-being refers to the being of desire, in accordance with the state of self-misrecognition in which the subject is installed by the signifying order.

Beyond this paradox of subjectivity, the imaginary problematics of the ego are such that, although it primarily concerns the subject, this construction in which he is alienated is not independent of the existence of the other. Because it is a projected image consisting of the subject's multiple representatives, *the ego can attain the status of imaginary representation only through the other and in relation to the other*. The mirror stage is a precursor of this dialectic. The child's identification with his mirror image is, in fact, possible only to the extent as it is sustained by a certain recognition from the Other (the mother).

> What is revealed in the triumph of the assumption of the body-image in the mirror is this object so evanescent that it appears only in the margins: the mutual gaze, evident in the fact that the child turns back towards the one who is in some way helping him, even if only by being present in his game. [Lacan 1966a, p. 70]

The child recognizes himself in his own image only insofar as he senses that the other has already identified him with this image. He thus receives from the gaze of the other the confirmation that the image he perceives is indeed his. In this sense the gradual emergence of subjectivity in the mirror stage prefigures the way in which the ego, as an imaginary construction, is irreducibly dependent on the dimension of the other. Lacan stresses this point in radical formulations like the following: "There is no way of grasping anything whatsoever of the analytic dialectic if we do not assume that the ego is an *imaginary construction*" (Lacan 1954–1955, p. 243, emphasis added). Again, quite explicitly: "The ego we are speaking of is absolutely impossible to distinguish from the *imaginary captations* that constitute it from head to foot, in its genesis as in its status, in its function and in its actuality, *by another and for another*" (Lacan 1954, p. 374, emphasis added). And a final passage: "The only homogeneous function of consciousness is in the *imaginary capture* of the ego by its mirror reflection and in the function of misrecognition that remains attached to it" (Lacan 1960a, p. 832, emphasis added).

In addition to the explicit reference that these three passages make to the imaginary relation of the subject with his ego, they may also imply that the relationship of the ego to the other is in a way analogous to the relationship between language [*langage*] and speech. This analogy illustrates the fundamental problem of the alienation of the subject in the ego as a consequence of the accession to language, as Lacan (1954–1955) analyzes it in his famous *Schema L of the intersubjective dialectic*.[2]

---

2. Schema L also appears in a simplified form in Lacan 1955–1956 (Sheridan 1977, p. 193):

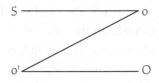

Translators' note: "Es" in the upper left-hand corner of the schema is the name of the letter "S" that stands for "Subject"; it is also the German word *Es*,

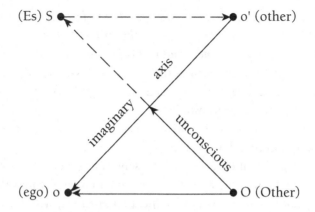

S is the subject, the subject in "his ineffable, stupid existence" as Lacan (Sheridan 1977, p. 194) describes it. In other words, this is the subject, caught in the net of language, who does not know what he is saying. But although the subject is in position S, it is not here that he apprehends himself: "He sees himself in *o*, and that is why he has an ego. He may believe that this ego is himself; everybody is at that stage, and there is no way of getting out of it" (Lacan 1954–1955, p. 243, translation modified).

Here we find an implicit reference to the mirror stage and the achievement of identity through an image, at first experienced as the image of an other and then assumed as one's own. Because the subject starts with the image of the other in acceding to his identity, he will enter into a subjective movement

---

meaning "it," i.e., the id. I am using *o*, *o*', and *O* (for the permutations of "other") where some translators retain Lacan's *a*, *a*', and *A* (for French *autre*, "other"), because it is particularly important to keep in mind the "otherness" of all these positions in Lacanian theory. Lacan characterized the lower left position indifferently as *o* or *o*', since the specular other and the ego are in effect interchangeable on the imaginary axis *oo*'. Regardless of the notation, the lower left position is that of the ego (the "me" in French), the upper right position that of the other.

correlative with the other. Thus *it is in the form of the specular other (the subject's own image in the mirror) that the subject will also perceive the other, that is, his fellow being,* situated at *o'* in the schema. "This form of the other has a very close relation to his ego; it can be superimposed on the ego, and we write it as *o'*" (p. 244, translation modified).

The subject's relation with himself is therefore always mediated by a fictional line, the axis *oo'.* The relation of S to *o* (ego) is thus dependent on *o'*, and, inversely, the subject's relation to the other (*o'*), his fellow being, is dependent on *o.* We may therefore speak of a *dialectic of identification of oneself with the other and of the other with oneself.* This is the context in which we are to understand Lacan's reference to Hegel, concerning the ego.

> In other words, the dialectic that supports our experience, located on the most enveloping level of the subject's efficacy, obliges us to understand the ego from one end to the other in the movement of progressive alienation where self-consciousness is established in Hegel's phenomenology. [Lacan 1954, p. 374]

The fourth term of Schema L is symbolized by *O*, the Other. Besides the symmetrical plane of the ego and the other, there is, as it were, a secant plane *O* → S that Lacan calls the *wall of language.* To understand this term, we first must clarify what happens when the subject addresses an other.

> When the subject speaks to his fellow beings, he speaks in the common language that holds the imaginary egos to be things that are not simply *ex-sistent*[3] but real. Since he can-

---

3. In writing "ex-sist" and "ex-sistant," Lacan metaphorizes the status of the subject with regard to his discourse. The prefix *ex-* and the Latin root *sist-* refer to the position of the subject as, in effect, always being "placed outside of."

not know what is in the domain in which the concrete dialogue takes place, he is dealing with a certain number of
characters, o', o''. Insofar as the subject brings them into relation with his own image, those with whom he is speaking
are also those with whom he identifies. [Lacan 1954–1955,
p. 244, translation modified]

When a subject communicates with another subject, communication, ("the common language") is always mediated by the
imaginary axis oo'. In other words, because of the division produced by language, when a true subject speaks to another true
subject what happens is that an ego is communicating with an
ego that is other, but similar to him. The result of this is that
speaking to an other inevitably amounts to holding a dialogue
of the deaf. The mediation of language that obscures the subject
therefore rules that, when S addresses himself to a true Other,
he never reaches him directly. This true Other is in effect situated on the other side of the *wall of language*, just as the subject
S himself is separated from his truth as a subject by this same
order of language.

We in fact address O_1's, O_2's, who are what we don't know,
true Others, true subjects.
They are on the other side of the wall of language, there
where in principle I never reach them. Fundamentally, *they*
are the ones I'm aiming at every time I utter true speech, but
I always reach oo' through reflection. I always aim at true
subjects, and I have to be content with shadows. The subject is separated from the Others, the true ones, by the
wall of language. [Lacan 1954–1955, p. 244, translation
modified]

The dialectic of intersubjectivity, even if it presupposes a
true Other whose existence must be posited in order to found

the discourse of the speaking subject, ends up as an imaginary exchange between two egos.

> If speech is founded in the existence of the Other, the true one, language is so made as to return us to the objectified other, to the other whom we can make anything we want of, including thinking that he is an object, that is to say that he doesn't know what he's saying. When we use language, our relation with the other always plays on this ambiguity. In other words, language is as much there to found us in the Other as to prevent us radically from understanding him. [Lacan 1954–1955, p. 244, translation modified]

The entire question of the alienation of the subject ("I") in and by language is played out to the advantage of the imaginary order of the ego. As Lacan (1954–1955) remarks, "The subject doesn't know what he is saying, and for the best of reasons, because he doesn't know what he is" (p. 244).

This structural consequence makes possible a precise conceptualization of the experience of analytic treatment, establishing what is undoubtedly the firmest foundation for the *return to Freud* at the central point of his discovery. "The analysis," says Lacan (1954–1955),

> must aim at the passage of true speech, joining the subject to an other subject, on the other side of the wall of language. That is the final relation of the subject to a genuine Other, to the Other who gives the answer one doesn't expect, which defines the terminal point of the analysis. [p. 246]

The analytic experience is thus suspended on the passage from *empty speech*—mediated by the imaginary axis *oo'*—to *full speech* to *true speech*. This is the crucial meaning of analysis for

Lacan, and the realization of its basic objective. He explains his view fully in this authoritative passage:

> Throughout the course of the analysis, on the sole condition that the ego of the analyst agrees not to be there, on the sole condition that the analyst is not a living mirror but an empty mirror, what happens happens between the ego of the subject and the others. The entire development of the analysis consists in the progressive displacement of this relation, which the subject can grasp at any moment, beyond the wall of language, this being the transference that is from him and in which he doesn't recognize himself. . . . The analysis consists in getting him to become conscious of his relations, not with the ego of the analyst, but with all those Others who are his true interlocutors and whom he hasn't recognized. It is a matter of the subject's gradually discovering which Other he is truly addressing without knowing it, and of his gradually assuming the transferential relations at the place where he is, and where at first he didn't know he was. [Lacan 1954–1955, p. 246, translation modified]

Freud's famous formula *Wo Es war, soll Ich werden* is evident here, in the sense in which Lacan understands it. In accordance with his idea of the aim of analysis, Lacan proposes to replace the unfortunate translation: "Where the id was, there the ego should be," (that is, the ego must dislodge the id) with: "Where the S was, there the *Ich* should be" (p. 246).[4] In other words, it is not the ego that should take precedence over the id. An analysis that aimed at such an outcome would be in collu-

---

4. Translator's note: The reader should keep in mind the French equivalents of Freud's *Ich and Es* (English "ego" and "id"), namely *moi* and *ça* ("me" and "that"), and recall that *Ich* is also the subject pronoun "I."

sion, according to Lacan, with the strategies of "ego strengthen-ing" dear to Ego Psychology and to other psychological regimens based on normative and educational assumptions. For Lacan, in contrast, the ego must progressively give precedence to the *Es*. But "this *Es*," he specifies, "take it as the letter *S*. It is there, it is always there. It is the subject" (p. 246). Hence the imaginary of the ego must give way, in analysis, to the subject in the authen-ticity of his desire, the truth of which is far too compromised by the alienation of the subject in the locus of his splitting.

In the light of Schema L, we can go back to the question of this alienation to try to determine its characteristics. These can be seen in the development of didactic knowledge in which the subject of the unconscious is foreclosed.

The alienation of the subject occurs, in Schema L, on the axis $o \rightarrow o'$. Separated from himself by the order of language, the subject is represented in the form of a stand-in functioning as o in the position of the ego. The ego can therefore take himself for the "I" (for the subject). In other words, the subject of the utterance is the subject imaginarily summoned to the place of the ego, where he is alienated without knowing it. Under these conditions, if the "suture" expresses "the relation of the subject to the chain of his discourse" (Miller, p. 39), we can specify its range according to the degree of alienation of the subject through the ego.

Lacan's theories do indeed make it possible to show that, depending on the forms of articulation of discourse, the real subject appears more or less gagged in this subject of the utter-ance who represents him. Certain strategies of discourse are quite radical in the way they evict the subject of the unconscious. This is particularly evident in all the strategies of rational discourse, and, *a fortiori*, in scientific, mathematical, and logical discourses, where the subject of the utterance completely deludes himself into thinking he is the subject as such. *Foreclosure of the subject* is the name given to this type of alienation of the authentic subject in favor of a privileged stand-in designated, for the occasion, as the *knowing subject* or the *subject of knowledge*.

The rational activity of the knowing subject in a way legislates the truth of things and even the truth of the subject himself. Because he takes it upon himself to put forward such true (or false) utterances, this knowing subject acquires the status of *epistemic subject*. This epistemic subject, decreeing by himself and for himself what true knowledge is, deludes himself about his truth only insofar as he uses discursive tools appropriate for this purpose. And such tools adequately ensure the displaying of positive knowledge only because they neutralize the subject of the unconscious. For this reason, the epistemic subject inevitably holds sway in the locus of the ego. His is the *nec plus ultra* of the imaginary performances of the ego, which culminate in discursive paradigms totally constrained by a certain ideal regarding both the subject and the goal he is pursuing. For the subject, this ideal is that of the transcendental subject (in the Kantian sense of the term, i.e., in reference to the *a priori* conditions of knowledge). As to the goal, the prospect is that of absolute knowledge. And so these two ideals find their best expression in the rationalism of science. In scientific discourse there is a maximum degree of suture because it is there that the subject of the unconscious is most effectively gagged. We can go even further and examine the type and the epistemological structure of this stifling gag in different scientific fields to show, as I have tried to do (Dor 1982 a,b), the nature of the parameters involved in the foreclosure of the subject.

19

Dialectic of Consciousness and Dialectic of Desire

In addition to the primary identification of the mirror stage, which echoes the Hegelian dialectic of consciousness presupposed in Schema L, Lacan sees the dynamics of desire as entirely organized in this same dialectical movement. Desire is always fundamentally structured as "desire of the Other's desire." We therefore need to review the major features of the dialectic of consciousness and desire discussed by Hegel (1907) in the *Phenomenology of Spirit*.

Schema L shows that the subject S apprehends himself only at *o*, that is, as an ego. Now the ego comes into being for the subject through *identification with his specular image*—in relation either to his own image in the mirror or to the image of someone like him. The subject's relation to himself is thus dependent on *o* and *o'*, so that we may speak of a genuine *dialectic of identification of oneself with the other and of the other with oneself.* This brings us to the Hegelian dialectic.

For Hegel, the dialectic of consciousness is an attempt to understand the developing process of the subject's relation to himself. He situates the origin of this movement in *immediate presence to self*, or what he calls *primal identity*. What we have here is the starting point in the process, when consciousness has not yet entered into relation with itself: this is the *in-itself of consciousness*.

THE FIRST PHASE

The first phase of the dialectic is a process of *separation of the self from itself*. This movement of *exteriorization* is essential if consciousness is to be able to enter into relation with itself, that is, to become self-consciousness.

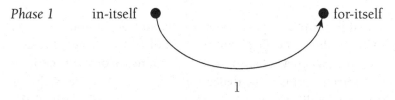

Phase 1   in-itself ●   ● for-itself

1

    Consciousness, then, first places itself at a distance from itself as object, and it is only through this self-objectification that it can be conscious of something external to itself. This something is the for-itself, and so this first phase is that of the *self-objectification of the for-itself*.

    For Hegel the alienation of the spirit outside of itself begins here in this initial phase. At the end of the process of exteriorization consciousness takes its own objectification as a given objectification, since the for-itself is an object exterior to consciousness in-itself. Thus, in a way, the alienation of consciousness begins at a time when consciousness is not yet aware that this objectivity is itself.

THE SECOND PHASE

In the first phase consciousness entered into a relation with itself. The second phase is a *movement of return*, a *reflexive movement*.

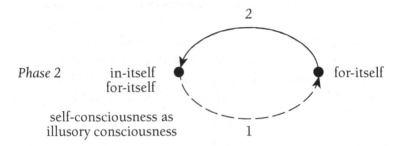

As a result of this return, consciousness has become *self-consciousness*, since from now on it apprehends itself as for-itself in itself; that is, as for itself in that it is in itself. This is the *for-itself in-itself* of consciousness, because it has consciousness of an object outside itself (for-itself) that is itself. We might think that at the end of this second phase consciousness has succeeded in establishing itself as self-consciousness, but this is not the case. For Hegel self-consciousness for-itself in-itself is the classic example of illusory consciousness in that it is still radically subjective. As such it once again bears witness to its alienation, since at the end of the second phase consciousness is certain *that there is no objectivity independent of itself.*

Consciousness for-itself in-itself, then, is a subjectivity that excludes any positive relation to objectivity, that is, to an object independent of a consciousness that thinks it. A third phase is necessary for the emergence from this illusory consciousness.

THE THIRD PHASE

At the end of the second phase, self-consciousness does not consciously know what it is. To be sure, it is consciousness for-itself, but it is for-itself only in-itself. In order to emerge from illusion, consciousness must redo this double movement if the relation to self is to become genuine self-consciousness.

The subjectivity that has been established (for-itself in-itself) must therefore set itself once again objectively in front of itself and once again enter into a relation with itself. This is how it becomes objectively for itself what it had been only subjectively.

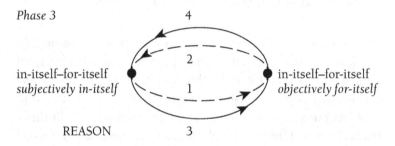

Phase 3   4

in-itself–for-itself   in-itself–for-itself
subjectively in-itself   *objectively for itself*

REASON   3

The third phase thus unfolds in a twofold process:

Process 3

Positing objectivity as objectivity (for-itself) of the subjectivity (self-consciousness).

Process 4

Positing subjectivity (self-consciousness) as subjectivity of the objectivity (for-itself).

At the end of Process 3, objectivity (for-itself) has become the self-conscious objectivity of subjectivity. At the end of Process 4, self-consciousness (in-itself for-itself) has become the subjectivity of its own objectivity. The achievement of self-consciousness is due to the fact that *consciousness has objectively established itself in-itself for-itself, that is, in-itself as for-itself, and for-itself as in-itself.* At this level of unity, consciousness achieves reason, so that we might say, with Hegel, that thought is the activity consisting in placing oneself in front of oneself in order to be for-oneself and to be oneself in this other self.

It is according to this dialectic process that there occurs recognition of the self by the other, and of the other by the self, as illustrated in Schema L.

For Hegel, mutual recognition is, from the outset, established dialectically in the dimension of desire and is subject to the advent of self-consciousness. To understand how this works, we must first define the status of the object in consciousness. As it happens, the notion of an object of consciousness is contradictory, in that such an object is simultaneously dependent on and independent of *this consciousness.*

In some respects, the consciousness that places itself outside of itself as object (for-itself) makes this object independent of itself. And indeed, in the self-objectification of the for-itself, the for-itself appears independent of the in-itself at the end of the first process. In other respects, however, this object is also dependent on consciousness, insofar as consciousness is self-consciousness only through the reflection in itself of this object. In other words, consciousness posits the independence of the object (for-itself) only in order to secure its dependence on it (for itself-in itself). It is in this sense that at the level of self-consciousness there is a contradiction with respect to the object.

It is only because of this contradiction that the essence of desire arises. Consciousness *never stops desiring the independence of the object, but does so only in order to further its own desire to establish itself as self-consciousness.* Thus, for Hegel, the essence of desire is contradictory by nature; it is based on the relation to something other than itself (for-itself) that must also be a relation to itself (for-itself in-itself). This explains why the relation to the other is also a relation to oneself, and the relation to oneself also a relation to the other. Consciousness is founded on a contradictory desire. The object must at one and the same time be other than consciousness (as consciousness for-itself), but also as it should be (i.e., as consciousness for-itself in-itself).

Through this contradictory requirement consciousness encounters a truth about the object of which it was not conscious at first. This truth is that *the object (for-itself) that consciousness establishes as independent of itself is also necessarily a self-consciousness, that is, another self that is self-consciousness.* And this must be so if consciousness is to recognize itself in this object as self-consciousness. However, it cannot discover this truth until it has related this object to itself, that is, until this object becomes a subject and consciousness discovers that this other, opposite it, is in fact itself.

This contradiction regarding the object and the truth consciousness discovers in it has a number of consequences. First, *the necessary existence of a multiplicity of self-consciousnesses* must be accepted. Second, the dimension of desire (of consciousness) inevitably appears as *desire of the other's desire.* Finally, consciousness *can recognize itself in the other only because the other recognizes itself in consciousness.*

If, in order to be constituted as self-consciousness, each consciousness must posit an object outside itself, and if this object necessarily proves to be another self-consciousness, it follows that *each consciousness, by positing an object outside it-self, desires to find a self-consciousness in that object.* When all is said and done, each consciousness desires to find an object that also desires. Therefore, *each consciousness desires to be desired through the object it desires.* In this sense, desire is always constituted as *desire of the other's desire.*

The dialectic of *reciprocal recognition* is based on this dialectic of desire. If desire is desire of the other's desire, this means that every consciousness desires to recognize itself in the other insofar as the other desires to recognize itself in it. This is where the dialectic of subjectivity occurs. I desire to recognize myself in the other. But since this other is me, this other me must recognize itself in me. I can recognize myself in this other me, therefore, only if I recognize that the other already recognizes himself in me; that is, if I recognize that I am the "me" of the other.

Hegel calls this problematics of reciprocal recognition *dual self-consciousness.* It is the basic principle of what Lacan brings into play in his theory of the mirror stage and in Schema L.

For Hegel, reciprocal recognition is best illustrated by the dialectic of master and slave. There is nothing human about man, in the beginning, except his status as living animal. As such, he is a mere creature of needs. To achieve his identity, he must become a being of desire, that is, a desiring consciousness or self-consciousness. In order to attain this self-consciousness, the living animal is obliged to do away with the other as living animal, since the advent of self-consciousness entails being able to recognize oneself in the other. But to carry out this process the converse must also be true: the other also must be able to recognize himself in the desiring consciousness. Thus the essence of desire is expressed in the fact that it is necessary for each being to find in the other another desiring consciousness. An inevitable *struggle to the death* ensues, in which each desires to annihilate the other as living animal in order to be able to find in him a desiring consciousness.

However, the only outcome of this struggle to the death is for it to become a *struggle for prestige*, since one of the two protagonists must surrender. In other words, the struggle to the death can end only in the establishment of a relationship of servitude. One of the combatants in effect stops fighting by showing the other that he fears death as a living creature and hence gives up the attempt to be recognized as self-consciousness. The master is thus recognized by the slave and *knows himself* to be so recognized. From this moment on, the process reverses itself, becoming the *dialectic of servile consciousness*.

The recognition of the master by the slave is unilateral and for this reason ineffective. The master is indeed recognized by the slave as self-consciousness, but he in no way finds himself as self-consciousness in the slave. He is thus recognized as self-consciousness by a consciousness that is not self-consciousness. For reasons that are analogous but reversed, the slave is no better able to recognize himself in the master. And yet the slave, as a consciousness, also aspires to recognition. He renounced this goal out of fear, but the desire to be an authentic self-consciousness remains. The slave is thus a consciousness for-itself in-itself, that is, a consciousness whose development was arrested at the stage of *illusory consciousness. This consciousness for-itself in-itself has not repositioned the for-itself in-itself objectively for itself and subjectively in itself.*

For the slave, recognition will be achieved through servile labor. The desire of the master is satisfied only by means of a consciousness that is recognized not as a desiring consciousness but as an enslaved one. For this reason, *the desire of the master is alienated from the consciousness of the slave.* Only the slave can give a human form to the object desired by the master. If this happens, then the slave gives a subjective sense to objectivity, and, in consequence, he simultaneously gives an objective sense to his own subjectivity. Under these conditions the for-itself becomes in-itself and the in-itself becomes for-itself. And this is how self-consciousness is authentically achieved.

In conclusion, then, it is clear that a being exists as self-consciousness only because the other exists as an opposed consciousness. The human individual thus recognizes himself as self-consciousness through the intermediation of the other. But to exist as self-consciousness, one must deny the other's existence as a desiring consciousness. The awareness of the desiring subject has meaning only insofar as it is opposed to another desiring consciousness from which it demands recognition. Desire is therefore established from the very start as the desire to be desired, as desire of desire—*desire of the Other's desire,* as Lacan calls it, using Hegel's formulation of this concept that, as analytic experience has shown, powerfully reveals the depth of human desire.

Part III

Desire—Language—The Unconscious

20

Need—Desire—Demand

Lacan established the metaphor of the Name-of-the-Father as a structural crossroads because it entails a host of metapsychological consequences linked to the inevitability of the division of the subject. With the acquisition of language, the speaking-being [*le parlêtre*] is constituted as a divided subject, and a part of his being is alienated in the unconscious that is a product of this very division. Fundamentally, the only outlet for the subject's desire is for that desire to become speech addressed to the other. The subject of desire, identified with the subject of the unconscious, is therefore hidden under the mask of the subject of the utterance, to whom this speech (what is said) seems to refer, and who can make himself understood by the other to whom this speech is addressed only in its enunciation (the act of saying).

The emergence of the subject thus leads to an irreversible intertwining, within him, of desire, language, and the unconscious, the structure of which is henceforth organized around the signifying order. We are now in a position to examine the elements of this intertwining in greater depth through the logic of Lacan's theoretical arguments. The starting point here is the distinction among *need*, *desire*, and *demand*, a distinction that structures the subject's unconscious desire in a special way. Desire tends to organize itself in relation to the other by means of what Lacan describes as the retroactive effect of demand on need. But it is because the subject first encounters his desire in a relationship to the other based on the intentionality of need that he will first experience his desire as *desire of the Other's desire*.

The problematics of desire, formulated by Lacan in relation to need and demand, can be fully understood only with reference to Freud's theory of the first experiences of satisfaction, in which Freud locates the essence of desire and the nature of its evolution (see Freud 1895, 1900, 1915a and Laplanche and Pontalis 1973).

Let us try, along with Freud, to imagine the psychic processes involved during these first experiences of satisfaction. First, we must not forget that the subject can be aware of a drive[1] only if it is expressed in the psychic apparatus by a representative. How, then, do the first satisfactions of the drives take place? For convenience's sake we will use the example of hunger. The drive initially manifests itself in the child by the appearance of displeasure caused by a state of tension inherent in the excitation of the drive. The child is in a situation of *need* requiring satisfaction. At this stage of the first experi-

---

1. Translator's note: In French, *pulsion* is used where English translations of Freud have either "drive" or "instinct." The author uses this single word where I have used one or the other of the English alternatives in the translation.

ence of satisfaction, the process is essentially organic. We must therefore conclude that the object given to the child to satisfy his need is given *without his looking for it* and without his having a mental representation of it. The drive process in this first experience of satisfaction comes under the heading of pure need, since the drive is satisfied without psychic mediation. Moreover, this process of satisfaction causes an immediate pleasure linked to the reduction in the state of tension inherent in the drive.

This first experience of satisfaction leaves a memory trace in the psychic apparatus, such that from now on satisfaction will be directly linked to the image/perception of the object that provided it. It is this memory trace that constitutes the child's representation of the drive process.

When the state of drive tension reappears, the memory trace will be reactivated. More precisely, it is the image/perception of the object and the memory trace of the process of satisfaction that are recathected. Thus, after the first experience of satisfaction, the drive process is no longer one of pure need. It is necessarily a need linked to a mnemic representation of satisfaction. During the next experience of satisfaction this representation, reactivated by arousal, will be identified by the child. But at first the child will confuse the mnemic evocation of the past satisfaction with the perception of the present event. In other words, he confuses the mnemic image linked to the primary experience of satisfaction with the identification of the present instinctual excitation. A confusion therefore exists between the *represented object* of the past satisfaction and the *real object* that can ensure satisfaction in the present, since, according to Freud, too great a cathexis of the mnemic image evokes the same index of reality as a real perception.

At first, then, the child tends to satisfy himself through hallucinatory satisfaction. It is only after successive repetition of experiences of satisfaction that the mnemic image will be distinguished from real satisfaction. Correlatively, the child will use this mnemic image to orient his search for the real object of satisfaction, insofar as he believes this real object of satisfaction to be like the mnemic image. Thus the mnemic image becomes the model of the object the child will look for in reality to satisfy the drive.

The mnemic image, then, functions in the psychic apparatus as a representation of anticipated satisfaction linked to the dynamics of the drive process. It is in this specific sense that we can speak of *desire* in psychoanalysis. Indeed, for Freud (1900), desire arises from recathexis of a mnemic trace of satisfaction linked to the identification of an instinctual excitation.

> The excitations produced by internal needs seek discharge in movement, which may be described as 'internal change' or 'an expression of emotion'. A hungry baby screams or kicks helplessly. But the situation remains unaltered, for the excitation arising from an internal need is not due to a force producing a *momentary* impact but to one which is in continuous operation. A change can only come about if in some way or other (in the case of the baby, through outside help) an 'experience of satisfaction' can be achieved which puts an end to the internal stimulus. An essential component of this experience of satisfaction is a particular perception (that of nourishment, in our example) the mnemic image of which remains associated thenceforward with the memory trace of the excitation produced by the need. As a result of the link that has thus been established, next time this need arises a psychical impulse will at once emerge which will seek to re-cathect the mnemic image of the perception and to re-evoke

the perception itself, that is to say, to re- establish the situation of the original satisfaction. *An impulse of this kind is what we call desire;*[2] the reappearance of the perception is the fulfillment of the desire; and the shortest path to the fulfillment of the desire is a path leading direct from the excitation produced by the need to a complete cathexis of the perception. [pp. 565–566, emphasis added]

Desire is thus irreducibly linked in a specific way to the instinctual process in which it is grounded. The recathexis of the mnemic image takes place through the mediation of an instinctual impulse, that is, an instinct in action (Laplanche and Pontalis 1973) appearing as a piece of information represented in the psyche as a result of instinctual excitation. It is because of the first association produced in the psyche that this recathexis of the mnemic image by the instinctual impulse becomes possible. This is therefore a dynamic process, since it can anticipate satisfaction in a hallucinatory manner. The very essence of desire is to be found in this dynamism. It is modeled on the first experience of satisfaction, and in subsequent experiences it orients the subject dynamically in the search for an object that can ensure this satisfaction.

We must therefore conclude that there is no satisfaction of desire in reality. Although conventionally we speak of desire as "satisfied" or "unsatisfied," the only reality of desire is a psychic one. It is the drive that may (or may not) find an object in reality that satisfies it, and it can do so precisely as a function of the desire that, as Freud emphasizes, impels the subject towards the object of the drive. However, *desire as such has no object in reality.*

---

2. Translator's note: Lacan and his followers translate Freud's term *Wunsch* ("wish") by *désir* ("desire"), and I have therefore modified the translation of this passage in accordance with Joël Dor's usage.

Lacan explains why it is that there is no real incarnation of the object of desire. He sees the dimension of desire as intrinsically linked to a *lack* that cannot be filled by any real object. The object of the drive, therefore, can only stand metonymically for the object of desire itself. Lacan's reflections on the Freudian concept of the drive enable him to clarify this notion of desire and to establish its dynamics in the context of the relation to the Other.

In *The Four Fundamental Concepts of Psychoanalysis*, Lacan (1964) examines the notion of the drive from the perspective of the four parameters Freud used to define it: source, thrust, aim, and object. He offers a series of illuminating observations on the nature of the connection linking desire and its object to the instinctual process.

After stressing the fact that Freud describes the drive not only as a "fundamental concept" but also as a "convention," Lacan begins by demonstrating that *drive must be distinguished from need*. While need is a rhythmic biological function, the drive, for Freud, is primarily dependent on a constancy of thrust. Moreover, whereas in Freud's view a drive is satisfied by the attainment of its aim, Lacan raises the problem of sublimation as an objection to this thesis. Sublimation is presented by Freud (1915a) as one of the possible destinies of an instinct, one in which the drive finds a satisfactory solution so that there is no need for repression. Yet, paradoxically, in sublimation the drive is inhibited with respect to its aim, which calls into question the idea of its satisfaction. It is this problem that leads Lacan (1964) to make a general remark on the meaning of instinctual satisfaction: *the drive is not necessarily satisfied by its object*.

> It is clear that those with whom we deal, the patients, are not satisfied, as one says, with what they are. And yet, we

know that everything they are, everything they experience, even their symptoms, involves satisfaction. They satisfy something that no doubt runs counter to that with which they might be satisfied, or rather, perhaps, they give satisfaction *to* something. They are not content with their state, but all the same, being in a state that gives so little content, they are content. The whole question boils down to the following—*what* is contented here? [p. 166]

Lacan then establishes more accurately the relationship between the instinctual process and the register of satisfaction by examining the status of the object. There is a radical difference between the object of need and the object of the drive: "For if one distinguishes, at the outset of the dialectic of the drive, *Not* from *Bedürfnis*, need from the pressure of the drive—it is precisely because no object of any *Not*, need, can satisfy the drive" (p. 167). In other words, the drive, trying out its object, discovers that it is not by this object that it is satisfied. Lacan notes, as an example, that what satisfies the instinct in the need for food is not the food itself but the "pleasure of the mouth." And he finds confirmation in Freud's text itself: "As far as the object of the drive is concerned, let it be clear that it is, strictly speaking, of no importance. It is a matter of total indifference" (p. 168, translation modified).[3]

---

3. Lacan is referring to the text that reads: "It may be changed any number of times in the course of the vicissitudes which the instinct undergoes during its existence" (Freud 1915a, pp. 122–123). Monique David-Ménard (1983) takes Lacan to task for misconstruing this passage: "Freud did not write that the object has, strictly speaking, no importance, nor that it is a matter of total indifference. Quite the contrary: its importance comes from the fact that it makes satisfaction possible, and does so to the extent that the subject can accept it in its variety. Lacan's misconstrual concerns the little word *beliebig*

If this is the case, then the object of a drive that might meet this condition cannot be the object of need. The only object having this property is the object of desire. This is the object that Lacan calls *objet a*:[4] it is, all at once, the *object of desire and the object that is the cause of desire—the lost object*. In this sense the *objet a*, because it is eternally lacking, designates the presence of a hollow that any object might fill. Thus, according to Lacan, such an object can find its place in the principle of instinctual satisfaction if we accept the idea that the drive goes around it in a circular course. The aim of the drive is therefore simply the return, in a circuit, of the drive to its source, and this is why an instinct can be satisfied without achieving its aim.

With Lacan's introduction of the object of desire and its place in the process of the drive—which is thereby differentiated from the register of need—we are brought to the radical dimension of desire, whose origin presupposes, above and beyond need, the presence of the Other. Lacan has made a major contribution to the post-Freudian development of the notion of desire with his theory that desire can arise only in a relation with the Other. It is in the realm of such an experience that desire finds the condition both of its genesis and of its inevitable repe-

---

("as much as one wishes," "at will"), which he replaces with "arbitrary," "indifferent." In Freud's text, *beliebig* is an adverb referring to another adverb (*oft*): the object changes *as often as one would like*. The nuance of arbitrariness does not imply the indifference of the object, but instead the need to change objects in order to attain sexual satisfaction." (Translator's note: I have translated from p. 205 of the French text here.)

4. Translator's note: I have retained the French term here, since it is commonly used in English translations of Lacan and in discussions of his work. The "*a*" stands for *autre*, the lower-case "other"; *objet a* is sometimes referred to as *objet petit a* (object "little" or "lower-case" *a*) to distinguish its referent from the *Autre*, the radically Other.

tition. More specifically, the dimension of desire will help to ensure that the child, prisoner of an organism dependent on the order of need, will move on from the stage of object to that of subject, since desire is inscribed only in the register of a symbolic relation to the Other, and through the Other's desire.

To return to the example of eating as the source of the first experiences of satisfaction, the newborn child is, by nature, dependent on the requirements of need. The first manifestations of these organic imperatives are characteristic states of physical tension constituting the response of the body to deprivation. The inability of the child to satisfy these organic requirements by himself calls for and justifies the presence of an other. How does the other assume responsibility for the child? The first thing to note is that these bodily manifestations immediately take on the value of *signs* for the other, since it is he who assesses and decides to understand that the child is in a state of need. In other words, these bodily manifestations have a meaning only insofar as the other ascribes one to them. We cannot, therefore, say that the child himself uses these bodily manifestations to *signify* something to the other. On the level of this first experience of satisfaction there is no intentionality on the part of the child, as if he were mobilizing his body in manifestations having the value of a message directed to the other. Yet these manifestations have an immediate meaning for the other, and this implies that the child is placed, from the very start, in a universe of communication in which the other's intervention constitutes a response to something originally taken to be a *demand*. Through his intervention, the other thus immediately refers the child to a semantic universe and a universe of discourse. In this respect, the other who inscribes the child in this symbolic frame of reference takes upon himself the role of privileged other for the child—the *Other*.

The mother, thus promoted to the rank of Other for the child, at the same time subjects him to the universe of her own signifiers once she provides food in response to the bodily manifestations that she had interpreted as a demand on the part of the child. And, in some way, we cannot but see this supposed demand as the projection of the Other's desire.

The primary experience of satisfaction continues when the mother "responds" by providing the needed object. With the assimilation of the object, the child's body reacts with an organic relaxation connected with the satisfaction of the need. The Other, once again, immediately gives a meaning to this phase of relaxation. And it is certainly because this meaning is supported by the desire the mother has invested in her child that the organic relaxation becomes, for her, a message the child is supposedly addressing to her as evidence of grateful recognition. In other words, *the child is inevitably inscribed in the universe of the Other's desire insofar as he is a captive of the Other's signifiers.*

The mother responds to the organic relaxation of the child's body with gestures and words that prolong the child's feeling of relaxation. This response causes the child to experience pleasure [*jouir*][5] above and beyond the satisfaction of his need. In this sense we can identify the locus of a global satisfaction in which the surplus of *jouissance* supported by the mother's love is backed up by the satisfaction of the need proper. It is only when the experience of satisfaction ends this way that the child

---

5. Translator's note: *Jouir* (verb) and *jouissance* (noun) are quasi-technical terms in Lacanian discourse, to be explained in detail in Volume 2. In ordinary French usage, they refer to enjoyment in the sense of enjoying property, rights, etc., as well as to pleasure in general and orgasmic sexual pleasure in particular. In accordance with customary practice, I shall leave *jouissance* untranslated, so that the reader may come to understand inductively its range of connotations for Lacan.

is in a position to be able to *desire through the mediation of a demand addressed to the Other.*

When the need reappears, the child can now use for himself the meaning that was given to the psychic experience of the first episode of satisfaction. This is the process described by Freud in which the emergence of desire depends on the reactivation of a mnemic trace during an instinctual excitation. The mnemic image recathected by the instinctual impulse flows, from now on, into an experience filled up by the signifying network of the Other. The dynamics of desire can therefore channel the stimulation of the body, under the influence of deprivation, into the organization of a system of signs that the child calls upon with increasing intentionality to address the Other, in expectation of renewed satisfaction provisionally assumed through hallucination. The signifying mobilization of the child's bodily manifestations thus forms a true *demand* for an urgently awaited satisfaction. This demand marks the beginning of the symbolic communication with the Other that will later reach its culmination in the paternal metaphor, in the mastery of spoken language. Through this demand the child marks his entry into the universe of desire that, as Lacan puts it, *is always inscribed between demand and need.*

If demand is above all an expression of desire, it is immediately twofold. Beyond the demand for satisfaction of need appears the demand for a "surplus" that is essentially a demand for love. In a general way, then, demand is always *formulated and addressed to others.* Even though it applies to an object of need it is basically "inessential," because it is a demand for love in which the child desires to be the sole object of desire of the Other who satisfies his needs. In other words, this desire of the Other's desire takes the form of the desire to "re-find" the original satisfaction in which the child was filled with a *jouissance* he had neither asked for nor expected. For the uniqueness of this *jouissance* lies in its immediacy in the primary experience of satisfaction, where the point is that it is *not* mediated by a demand. As a result, the mediation by demand in the second experience of satisfaction confronts the child with the register of loss. Something has, as it were, fallen away in the difference that is now experienced between what is given to the child without psychic mediation and what is given only with the necessary mediation of the demand.

The emergence of desire thus depends on the seeking and the "re-finding" of the primary experience of *jouissance*. However, with the second experience of satisfaction and from then on, the child is caught up in and subjected to meaning, and must express a demand in order to make his desire understood. He must try to *signify* what he desires. But the mediation involved in having to designate something by name introduces a discrepancy between what is fundamentally desired and what can make itself understood in the demand. It is this discrepancy that is the measure of the impossibility of re-finding the original *jouissance* with the Other. The Other who gave *jouissance* to the child is sought after and awaited, but remains out of reach, lost as such because of the break introduced by the demand.

And so the Other becomes *the Thing—das Ding—*whose desire the child desires; but none of the child's demands, on which this desire is supported, will ever be able to signify it adequately. In *The Ethics of Psychoanalysis* (1959–1960) Lacan interrogates the Thing and, in this connection, begins to formulate the problematics of desire as involving an impossible object. The Thing is *unnamable*, and its essence is doomed to an "impossible symbolic saturation" (Safouan 1968, p. 44) in that the very fact of designation confirms the impossible relation to it. The further demand extends, the wider becomes the distance from the Thing. From one demand to another, desire is therefore structured as a desire of an impossible object beyond the object of need, an impossible object that demand struggles to signify.

Desire is thus inevitably reborn identical to itself, grounded in the lack left by the Thing, so that *this void is as much the cause of desire as it is its aim*. The void marks off a space that can be occupied by any object, and such objects will always be mere substitutes for the missing object. In this sense the object of desire does not, strictly speaking, exist, except insofar as it is designated as the eternally missing object. Lacan calls this object that is at the same time the object that causes desire and the object of desire *objet a*. Because it bears witness to a loss, *objet a* is in itself a *lack-producing object*, since it is impossible to make up for this loss.

Desire, necessarily separated from need because it is above all *lack-of-being* [*manque à être*] beyond demand, places the child in a permanent relation to the Other's desire. It is because the child senses (rather than discovers) that the Other's desire is marked by the same lack as his own that he can constitute himself as a potential object of the Other's desire and even as the object that might fill the Other's lack by identification with the phallic object. In a way, being the sole object of the desire of the Other amounts to a challenge on the part of the child to the essence of desire, which is lack. Just as the child challenges this dimension of lack on his own behalf, he seeks to challenge it in the Other by presenting himself as the object of that lack. Conversely, recognizing the lack in the Other as impossible to satisfy indicates that the child accepts the lack in the process of his own desire. (Lacan symbolizes the recognition of the lack in the

Other by the formula S($\emptyset$), the signifier of the lack in the Other.)
This recognition is the very essence of the phallic stakes in the
oedipal dialectic. At the end of the oedipal stage the child gives
up his position as object of the Other's desire and assumes the
position of desiring subject, where he may choose substitute
objects of desire that metonymically take the place of the lost
object.

21

The Graph of Desire 1:
From the Anchoring Point
to the Chatterbox

The relation of the subject to his desire, grounded in lack, is in no way based on a pre-established harmony, since desire is always metonymic, desire of something other than what demand can convey. This is the paradox of desire. Although it has its basis *on this side* of demand, it is in demand that it finds signifying material so that it can express, *beyond* demand, the unconscious truth of the subject, which is therefore spoken without his knowing it.

Desire, forced to become speech in the mold of demand, is thus a prisoner of the process of language. However, because of its logical anteriority to the discursive sequence that actualizes it, all of language itself remains caught in the net of the unconscious determinants of desire. The most immediate evidence of this intertwining of desire, the unconscious, and language is the radically contingent character of meaning. The deployment of discourse by the speakingbeing [*parlêtre*] makes it inevitable that *there is no meaning in itself; the only meaning is a metaphorical one*. Meaning never emerges except from the substitution of one signifier for another in the signifying chain. In other words, the primacy of the signifier over the signified is what is most important. This is demonstrated in an anecdote Lacan (1957a) recounts:

> A train arrives at a station. A little boy and a little girl, brother and sister, are seated in a compartment face to face next to the window through which the buildings along the station platform can be seen passing as the train pulls to a stop: 'Look,' says the brother, 'we're at Ladies!' 'Idiot,' replies his sister, 'Can't you see we're at Gentlemen.' [p. 152]

This little restroom story, expressing the imperative by which man's "public life is subjected to the laws of urinary segregation" (p. 151), is a reminder that a signifier takes on meaning only through its inevitable reference to another signifier. The signifier cannot represent the signified. "Gentlemen" and "Ladies" are two different signifiers for the two children only insofar as they are associated with the same signified as a function of other signifiers.

We have already emphasized that this primacy of the signifier over the signified was, in Lacan's view, at the origin of a different concept of signifying segmentation from the one defined by Saussure (see Chapter 5). In addition to the fact that, for Lacan, signifying segmentation is presented as the immediate establishment of connection between a flux of signifiers and a flux of signifieds, it is by this segmentation that the endless sliding of signification is momentarily stopped. The *anchoring point* constitutes this process of segmentation, which recalls the function of the value of the sign in the process of signification.

> If we must find a way to get closer to the relation of the chain of signifiers to the chain of signifieds, it is through this rough image of the anchoring point. . . .

> It's quite clear, for example, that if I start a sentence
> you won't understand its meaning until I've finished it, since
> it's really quite necessary for me to have spoken the last
> word of the sentence if you are to understand where its first
> one was. [Lacan 1957–1958, seminar of November 6, 1957]

Although the anchoring point replaces the Saussurian *cut*,
its implications go far beyond the principle of linguistic segmentation that determines the sign for the founder of structural linguistics. Lacan's introduction of the anchoring point highlights
a dimension of the process of speech that we might call pre-
linguistic: the dimension of desire. And this is why the topo-
graphical representation of this segmentation, the anchoring
point, is at the very basis of the *Graph of Desire*.

The Graph of Desire was gradually developed by Lacan in
the course of two successive seminars: *"Les formations de l'inconscient"* ["The Formations of the Unconscious"] (1957–1958) and
"Le Désir et son interprétation" ["Desire and its Interpretation"]
(1958–1959). He refers to the basic schema once again in "Subversion of the Subject and the Dialectic of Desire in the Freudian Unconscious" (1960b).

The basic constitutive element of the graph is given in the
following schema, which plots the anchoring point.

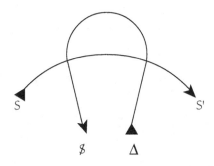

Vector $\overrightarrow{\Delta\$}$ represents the anchoring operation, the pinning down of the signifying chain represented by vector SS'. $\overrightarrow{\Delta\$}$ is thus the *vector of the signifieds*. The metaphor of anchoring characterizes a double intersection that illustrates a specific property of discourse, namely that it is from the last term of a spoken sequence that the first one and those that follow derive their meaning. In other words, the backwards movement of the anchoring vector $\overrightarrow{\Delta\$}$ is a metaphor, on the above graph, for the value of the Saussurian sign, that is, the determination of meaning retroactively, "each term being anticipated in the construction of the others, and, inversely, sealing their meaning by its retroactive effect" (Lacan 1960b, p. 303). The retroaction illustrated by the reverse movement of anchoring thus takes into account the most salient lesson of analytic experience concerning the discourse of the "speakingbeing."

Although the anchoring point clearly demonstrates the principle of the link between the signified and the signifier in the process of language, this link cannot be reduced to a simple process of intersection such as we find on the above graph. Lacan (1957–1958) presented a more structured version of it, and it is to this one that we shall refer from now on. Here, once again, is the graphic representation of the anchoring point. Remember that the mark ▲ always represents the beginning of the trajectory, and the arrow represents its end:

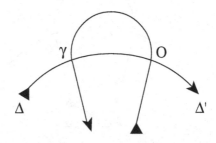

In this new figure, the signifying chain is represented by the vector $\overrightarrow{\Delta\gamma O\Delta}$'.

Because of the primacy of the signifier over the signified, this chain is a favorable site for metaphoric and metonymic operations, since, as we have previously seen, metaphors and metonymies are always based on substitutions of signifiers.

Moreover, this vector $\overrightarrow{\Delta\gamma O\Delta}$' is substantially made up of *phonemes*, that is, of the smallest linguistic units, without meaning, whose combination produces signifiers. Each language consists of a definite but limited number of these minimal distinctive units that are easy to discern by switching two of them in the same context of a spoken sequence. If the substitution produces two different meanings, we are dealing with phonemes.

Example: "He has a bat" / "He has a bag"

The commutation of /t/ and /g/ produces two different meanings, and thus /t/ and /g/ are authentic phonemes. In other words, phonemes are specified by the code of each language, and it is by the system of phonemic opposition that messages can be distinguished from one another. Because of its phonemic structure, vector $\overrightarrow{\Delta\gamma O\Delta}$' can therefore potentially actualize a multitude of signifying effects.

The representation of the anchoring point is completed by a new circuit, Oββ'γ.

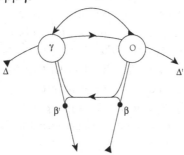

This is the circuit or circle of rational discourse. This discourse, which is simply our habitual or common one, is made up of *semantemes*, that is, of signifying elements. Thus the circle of discourse determines the usage of signifiers, that is, of what, in the practice of a given discourse, constitutes the fixed points determined by the *code*.

The code is defined as the set of signs and symbols that allow both the representation and the transmission of information, which is possible only because this set of signs and symbols is governed by pre-established conventions. The code of the discourse authorizes as well as founds intersubjective communication.

Because of the rules of the code, the circle of discourse is a level of articulation of speech at which the possibilities for creation of meaning are very limited, since meaning is fixed by the code itself. Consequently, this circle is a locus of relatively empty discourse, of *empty speech*. It is the locus of the concrete discourse of the "speakingbeing" trying to make himself understood.

In this diagram the two vectors, drawn in opposite directions to show that they slide towards one another, intersect at two clearly identifiable points. The first, *point O, which is the point where the various uses of the signifiers are determined, is the locus of the code.* As such, point O is *the locus of symbolic reference*, of that to which discourse refers insofar as it is characterized by an intersubjective fitness distinguishing it from delusional discourse, which is not supported by this symbolic guarantor. *The locus of the code is therefore the locus of the Other with a capital "O,"* which is why Lacan calls it both the "treasure-house of signifiers" and the "companion of language."

The second point of intersection, *point γ*, where the loop ends, is the locus of the encounter with the signifying chain, where meaning will be formed from the code. It is thus the *locus of the message*. The message is a sequence of signals, of symbols that correspond to combinatory rules strictly determined by a code. The meaning of the message cannot be understood except as a function of this code, since, in the end, to perceive the meaning of a message is always to decode the form of a previously encoded message.

Because point γ is the locus of the message, it is also the place where something on the order of the truth of the speaker is most likely to emerge in the form of *full speech*. Now as Lacan observes, most of the time no truth emerges at the locus of the message, because discourse does not really cross the signifying chain. It passes on this side of it, short-circuiting the chain, avoiding the big loop $\overrightarrow{o'\gamma}$ that goes from the code to the message. It is because of this short-circuit, represented by the segment $\overrightarrow{\beta\beta'}$ on the graph, that a discourse can express absolutely nothing of this truth—it goes around and around in endless, idle droning. Through this circuit the "speakingbeing" makes his best effort, only to wear himself out in the register of the empty speech of what Lacan calls the *chatterbox*. This type of speech bears witness to our condition as speaking animals: "It's with the common discourse of these words that say nothing that we reassure ourselves that we are not faced with being in the role of merely what man is in his natural state, namely a ferocious beast" (Lacan 1957–1958, seminar of November 6, 1957).

The short-circuit of the chatterbox readily intersects these two specific points, β and β', since these points represent two essential agencies. Point β' is the locus of the *metonymic object*, that is, the object that always metonymically replaces the object of desire. As for point β, it denotes *the subject, the "I," the locus, in discourse, of the one who speaks.*

Now that we have reached this first stage in the elaboration of the Graph of Desire, it is possible to demonstrate some fundamental properties verified both by linguistic analysis and by psychoanalytic experience.

First, it is clear that a message—whatever it may be—cannot be formulated unless this system exists in its totality. Furthermore, a subject's authentic speech (full speech) can emerge at the locus of the message only because a signifying chain is deployed under the supervision of a code governing its usage. Consequently, *any subject who engages his discourse in the short-circuit of the "chatterbox" necessarily communicates much more than he counts on saying.* This surplus of meaning results from a signifying elaboration to be found in the upper part of the diagram, which, even though it has been excluded from the circuit, is nonetheless implicitly present.

We can demonstrate the mechanism of this creation of meaning by examining the functioning of the entire system in the context of a formation of the unconscious. For if the articulation of language is capable of creating meaning, it can do so only by means of metaphoric and metonymic processes, and, as we have seen, it is precisely these two processes that are the mechanisms of choice for the productions of the unconscious.

In his seminar *Les formations de l'inconscient* ["The Formations of the Unconscious"], Lacan (1957–1958) puts the functioning of his graph to the test using a formation of the unconscious that clearly illustrates the process of creation of meaning in language: the witticism "famillionaire" discussed by Freud (1905b).

Several supplementary points of theory must first be presented before we can understand the detailed analysis Lacan develops as he works out the mechanism of the joke on the graph.

It is especially important to explain more fully the nature of the reference to the Other that is fundamental to the process of communication. Specifically, this means being sure that, in communication, the code is isotopic with the locus of the Other, from which it follows that the unconscious is the discourse of the Other.

22

The Formula of Communication and the Unconscious as Discourse of the Other

In discourse the "I" is the locus where the subject appears as the one who is speaking. We have seen that this special circumstance is due to the nature of the subject: the subject emerges only *in* discourse and *through* discourse, if only to disappear immediately. This *fading*[1] of the subject is a result of the relation of the subject to his own discourse, as Lacan observes in connection with the fact that a signifier is what represents a subject for another signifier (see Chapter 16).

A fundamental consequence, one that we have not yet touched upon, arises from this structure of division, for we must mark the inevitable distinction in discourse between the locus where the discourse itself *originates* and the locus where *it is produced by being reflected there*. In other words, we have to examine the relation between the Other and the "I" in the articulation of discourse.

Here we must return to Schema L in order to look more closely at certain points left unresolved, in particular the direc-

---

1. Translator's note: The author uses the English word, as did Lacan.

tions of the different vectors that link the four terms of the schema, S, *o'*, *o*, and O.

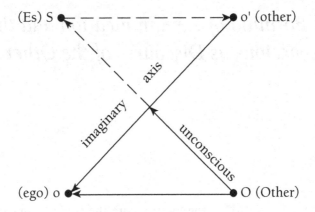

Let us briefly recall the way in which Schema L represents some of the consequences that structure communication (see Chapter 18). The subject S can never grasp himself except in the form of his *ego*, at *o*. The form his ego takes thus constitutes his identity; as the mirror stage demonstrates, it remains strictly dependent on the specular other. For this reason, the relation of the subject to himself and to others (his objects) is always mediated by the imaginary axis *oo'*. This is a relation of reciprocal influence, as the relation of the subject to his ego necessarily depends on the other, and, conversely, his relation to the other always depends on his ego. This dialectic of self to other and other to self leads to a unique mode of intersubjective communication. When a subject S tries to communicate with a subject O, he always misses his target, the authentic subject who is his interlocutor. Because of the imaginary axis *oo'* it is always an ego that communicates concretely with another similar ego. In other words, the S who speaks to the "Other with a capital O" can communicate only with an "*other* with a small o." In communication, the subject thus remains entirely a prisoner of the fiction into which his own subjective alienation has inserted him.

The direction of the arrows in Schema L shows the structure of this intersubjective communication. The subject S who addresses the Other encounters straightaway the other (S---→ o'), who sends him *ipso facto* back to his own ego (o' → o) along the axis of imaginary constructions of egos and alter egos. Lacan stresses the meaning of this necessarily reflexive relation: an ego is always an alter ego and vice versa.

As for the meaning of the other vectors, we can see that the vector going from O to S continues its trajectory in a dotted line after being intersected by o' → o (O— ---→ S). Another vector originating at O ends at the ego (O → o). This twofold vectorial orientation is, in appearance, contradictory to the previous orientations. It is as if, when a subject S addresses an Other, *something of this Other comes to him* from the mere fact that he is addressing him. But what comes to him from this Other comes in a peculiar manner characterized simultaneously by the mark of the reference to the unconscious and by the dotted line starting at the intersection with o' → o. It seems, therefore, that there is something coming from the Other that interferes with the very articulation of the subject's speech when he speaks to O. In the same way, something of the Other directly (solid line) collides with what is happening on the level of the ego (O → o).

Let us take Lacan's (1954–1955) advice in our analysis of these different vectors and "light up the magic lantern a little" (p. 323) through the use of an explanatory metaphor borrowed from the principle of electrical conduction. Imagine that Schema L is an electrical circuit with a triode lamp (a lamp with a cathode, an anode, and a transversal) at the point where the symbolic direction $\overrightarrow{SO}$ and the imaginary axis $\overrightarrow{o'o}$ intersect.

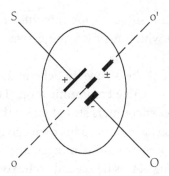

When current passes through the circuit, an electronic bombardment from the cathode to the anode is produced. If the transversal is positively polarized, the electrons will always be conducted towards the anode and the current will pass. If it is polarized negatively, however, the negative electrons coming from the cathode will be repelled by the negative and the current will no longer pass.

According to Lacan (1954–1955), this electronic metaphor shows exactly how the Imaginary (⊠) is able "to chop up, to scan,[2] what is happening on the level of the circuit." He adds that "what happens between O and S has an inherently conflictual character. At best, the circuit thwarts itself, halts itself, cuts itself off, chops itself up" (p. 323, translation modified). We must keep this in mind when we consider the subjective circuit of speech.

Given this conflict inherent in the symbolic direction, can we nevertheless conceive of a way in which a subject could produce speech that might be considered fundamental speech? In other words, can there be *full speech*, authentic communication between S and O? Such communication, unimpeded by the

---

2. Translator's note: "Scan" is used in the sense of dividing verse into metrical units.

imaginary interferences of $o' \rightarrow o$, would be proof that speech addressed to an Other who is not an other can exist. This possibility depends on the answer to the apparently banal question What is speech?—namely Lacan's (1955–1956) succinct formulation, "To speak is first of all to speak to others" (p. 36). It is this that, according to Lacan, allows us to make the radical distinction between speech and the mere recording of language.

Schema L enables us to understand what "to speak to others" means. A subject speaking to another always addresses a message to this other whom he necessarily takes to be an Other; this other to whom he is speaking is recognized as an absolute Other, a genuine subject. But even if the subject recognizes him as Other, Lacan (1955–1956) adds, *he does not know him as such,* because "it's essentially this unknown in the otherness of the Other that characterizes the speech relation at the level at which speech is spoken to the other" (p. 38).

In true speech, therefore, the Other is that by which we are recognized to the same extent that we have already implicitly recognized it as such. And it must be so in order for us, ourselves, to be recognized as the bearers of full speech. As Lacan (1955–1956) emphasizes, this presupposes

> recognition of an absolute Other, aimed at beyond all you can know, for whom recognition is to be valued only because it is beyond the known. It is through recognizing it that you institute it, and not as a pure and simple element of reality, a pawn, a puppet, but as an irreducible absolute, on whose existence as subject the very value of the speech in which you get yourself recognized depends. [p. 51]

The impulse behind the articulation of full speech is therefore given to us by the very principle structuring authentic communication in the type of message that the subject structures as

if it were coming from the other in an inverted form. This is
another way of saying that the sender receives his own message
back from the receiver in an inverted form.

The same is true for basic formulas such as "You are my
master" or "You are my wife," messages that, when one is speaking *fully* in the strict sense of the term, mean the converse of
what they express at the moment they are spoken and thus clearly
illustrate the Other's implicit recognition. Hence the subject
addressing the Other in "You are my master" is implicitly telling him: "I am your disciple," even though what he says in reality at that moment is still "You are my master." It is because the
subject has already gotten himself implicitly recognized as a
disciple in regard to the Other that he can explicitly recognize
this Other as his master in his speech. This structure of communication is imperative, because it alone explains the authoritative certainty with which the subject affirms "You are my
master." As Lacan (1955–1956) points out,

> *You are my wife*—after all, what do you know about it? *You
> are my master*—in point of fact, are you so sure? Precisely
> what constitutes the foundational value of this speech is that
> what is aimed at in the message . . . is that the other is there
> as absolute Other. [p. 37, translation modified]

The assurance that the subject brings to "You are my master" can in fact be grounded only in a realm beyond his speech—
indeed, to put it more precisely, *in a message that he has already
received from this "beyond"* and by means of which he has already
recognized himself as a disciple.

> The *You are my wife* or *You are my master* means—*You are
> what is still within my speech, and this I can affirm only by
> speaking in your place. This comes from you, to find there the*

certainty of what I pledge. This speech is speech that commits you. The unity of speech insofar as it founds the position of the two subjects is made apparent here. [Lacan 1955–1956, pp. 36–37, translation modified]

The "beyond" of speech where this implicit message comes from is thus the Other, and this is why human language depends on a form of communication in which our message comes to us from the Other in an inverted form (Lacan 1966b, p. 9). This is another way of saying, with Lacan (1953), that "speech always subjectively includes its own reply" (p. 85). It is as though to address someone were already to reply to him; we might say that in authentic communication speaking amounts to making the Other, as such, speak.

This influence of the Other in the process of intersubjective communication is presented in Schema L. As we can see from the direction of vector O— ---→ S, the speech that subject S addresses to the Other already comes to him from O in an inverted form. But this message from O, because it is implicit, comes to S without his knowing it; this is why *unconscious* is written along the symbolic axis that starts at O and ends at S. Vector O$\overrightarrow{o}$ indicates that, although it is there, the message coming from the Other escapes the subject. Subject S, addressing the Other, hears himself say at point *o* (the point of imaginary representation of the speaking subject), "You are my master." "I am your disciple," the message originally constituted at O, reaches him in the inverted form "You are my master" only because of the mediation of the imaginary axis *o'* → *o*. (This is why vector OS is drawn with a dotted line after the intersection with axis *o'* → *o*.) In this sense, it is clear that at the locus of the ego (*o*) the articulation of the message is totally overdetermined by the message coming from O (O → *o*).

The *wall of language* described by Lacan is this obstruction that hinders direct communication between subjects. Consequently, we can posit the unconscious as "this discourse of the Other where the subject receives, in an inverted form suited to the promise, his own forgotten message" (Lacan 1957b, p. 439). In "The Direction of the Treatment and the Principles of its Power" Lacan (1958) sums up the full impact of addressing another in speech.

> Let's set out again with these notions: that first of all, for the subject, his speech is a message because it is produced in the locus of the Other. And because of this, even his demand originates there and is formulated as such. This is not only because it is subject to the code of the Other, but also because it is dated from this locus (and even from the time) of the Other. [p. 269, translation modified]

As ultimate proof of this structure of speech, we may refer to a clinical case that provides *a contrario*, by the intrusion of psychotic speech, the evidence for the existence of the Other as guarantor of the symbolic reference.

This vignette, reported in the seminar *The Psychoses* (Lacan 1955–1956), came from a clinical case presentation of Lacan's, in the course of which a paranoid woman volunteered the account of the following incident to him.

As she was leaving home one day, abuse was hurled at her by a lewd and very ill-mannered man, the lover of her friend next door. This man said a coarse word to her that she could not, at first, bring herself to repeat. It would seem, however, that the coarse word did not come about unprovoked. She admitted that she herself had mumbled some thoughtless comments to him as he passed by: "I've just been to the pork-butcher's."

Lacan deduced that there must have been an allusion to pork or pig in what she had said to this vulgar person. But why was it in the form of an allusion that this opinion of him was expressed? Why did she say, "I've just been to the pork-butcher's" and not simply "Pig"? The mystery cleared up a bit when she confessed that, after her remark, the vulgar person had answered "Sow," which was the coarse word she had at first not been able to utter. Lacan immediately saw here an example of the formula of communication—the subject receives his message from the Other in an inverted form. In the present case, however, this was quite an unusual form of communication, since the message came to the psychotic woman from an *other* who was not the *Other*. It is a distinctive feature of psychotic speech that the anticipated and inverted message does not come from the locus of the *Other*.

On the one hand, Lacan points out, it certainly seems as if "sow" were the subject's own message reflected back at her. But this structure of communication can be fully confirmed only in the light of the subject's pathology. This case involved a typical form of paranoia that took the form of a *folie à deux* shared by a mother and daughter. These two symbiotically linked women had a solitary relationship, an existence cut off from the external world. Even though the daughter had married, she could not separate herself from her mother and vice versa. The dramatic course of her marriage only reinforced this pathological closeness—indeed, at one point the mother–daughter couple had had to flee the outbursts of the husband, who threatened to cut his wife into slices. From that moment on, Lacan notes, the two women organized their life in total exclusion of the male element, a foreign element to be rejected forever. It was in this exclusively female world that a discourse was structured in such a way that the two women were no longer in a position to receive their message from the other; they could articulate it only themselves, to one another. This type of communication that they had established between themselves was thus projected onto everyone else, without exception.

Under these conditions, the insult could only be a defense mechanism that arose in their relationship by means of a reflexive discourse. If speech is structured so that it is always the Other who speaks behind us, in the present case of the offensive word, who said "sow"? According to Lacan, it was as if the encounter with the vulgar man had triggered the auditory hallucination of the word "sow," which came as a reply to "I've been to the pork-butcher's." Precisely because this was a hallucination, the patient assumed that the neighbor's lover was something real that spoke. And so it was from this *other* that was like her that her own speech came back to her. In other words the message here did not truly arrive in an inverted form, since it was her own speech that was *in* the other. Speech articulated in the Real does not come from a "beyond" of the partner who is the Other; it comes from a "beyond" of the subject himself, which is not the "beyond" of the symbolic reference but a purely subjective one. In this sense, the entire pattern of communication tends to invert itself and hence to be deployed in the manner of delusional speech. Lacan concludes that it is no longer the address articulated as the reply to a message coming from the Other. From this imaginary "beyond," on the contrary, it is the reply that both presupposes and prompts the address. Here, it is "sow" that determines "I've just been to the pork-butcher's."

We can clearly explain the dynamics of this delusional communication by referring to Schema L.

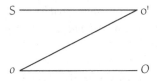

Let us locate the neighbor's lover at *o'* and the subject's ego at *o*. In the present case, O has been completely excluded from the circuit. It is at *o* that the message coming from S is articulated at the level of the ego in the form "I've just been to the pork-butcher's." But it is the vulgar person, *o*'s alter ego, who is *thought* to have uttered the offensive "sow" at *o'*. The person speaking does, therefore, in a way receive her own message in an apparently inverted form coming from *o'*, that is, from the other. What she says thus has to do with the "beyond" of what she herself is as a subject. But here the subject S is not really addressing O, who remains out of the circuit. She is addressing *o'*, from whom she receives her own words, but without realizing that "her own speech is in the other who is herself, the lower-case other, her reflection in her mirror, her counterpart" (Lacan 1955–1956, p. 51, translation modified). Thus, as Lacan notes, in this delusional speech "the circuit closes on the two small others who are the puppet opposite her, which speaks, and in which her own message resonates, and herself who, as an ego, is always an other and speaks by allusion" (p. 52).

Lacan emphasizes that the structure of the allusion is blatantly obvious in that she does not know what she is saying about herself.

> Who has just been to the pork-butcher's? A cut-up pig. She doesn't know that she's saying this, but she says it nevertheless. That other to whom she's speaking, she says to him about herself: *I, the sow, have just been to the pork-butcher's,*

I am already disjointed, a fragmented body, membra disjecta, *delusional, and my world is fragmenting, like me.* [p. 52, translation modified]

In conclusion, this example shows that in delusional speech everything that concerns the speaking subject is really said in the place of the *other*, because the *Other* is excluded from the circuit of speech. But this exclusion also excludes that which establishes and guarantees the truth of full speech in the discourse of the subject.

23

The Graph of Desire 2: The Creation of Meaning in the Signifying Technique of the Joke and the Subversion of the Unconscious in Language

Beyond the short-circuit of the "chatterbox" as it was introduced on the first level of the elaboration of the graph (see Chapter 21), the signifying articulation can nonetheless give rise to full speech. It can still do so, for example, by means of an unconscious formation that produces an authentic effect of creation of meaning. The example of the witticism *famillionaire* clearly shows this technique of the signifier as we see it worked out on the graph.

We have called attention to the structural correlations between the process of working out jokes and the process of metaphoric–metonymic constructions (see Chapter 9). Lacan reminds us that, from the outset, Freud adopted a structural theory of the signifier in regard to understanding jokes. Moreover, if the joke is above all the product of a "technique of the signifier," it follows that what we are dealing with is a technique in which the signified plays a secondary role. This is obvious from the construction of the neologism *famillionaire* on the graph.

Let us briefly recall that the context in which this famous witticism arose was the attempt of Hirsch-Hyacinth to describe the way Salomon Rothschild had greeted him. He had originally intended to say: "He treated me as an equal, on totally familiar terms," but instead he said: "He treated me on totally famil-lionaire terms." Freud immediately spotted the mechanism of condensation in the construction of this neologism:

FAMILI   AR

MILLIONAIRE

FAMILLIONAIRE

Let us go back to the first representation of the graph to show the mechanism that brought about this kind of "stamping" (Lacan 1957–1958) between two signifying lines:

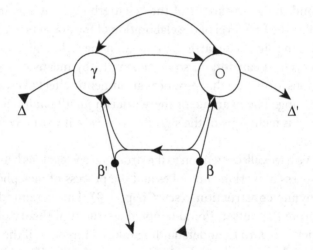

The circuit of speech *apparently* originates at β, the place where the subject is produced as the one who speaks. But structurally, as we have seen, the true point of departure of speech is at O, the locus of the Other where the subject receives his own message in an inverted form. As a result, the actual circuit of speech originates at O on the graph (in the locus of the Other). It is then reflected at β—which is thus the place of the "I"—and then comes back towards O (the place of the code) and extends out towards γ, where the message is completed.

If Hirsch-Hyacinth had actually said, "He treated me as an equal, on totally familiar terms," the circuit of this discourse would have been $\overrightarrow{O\beta}$, and $\overrightarrow{\beta O}$ and $\overrightarrow{O\gamma}$. In other words, it is at O, the locus of the code, that a listener could have understood such a phrase. But, as Lacan emphasizes, it is because of the mysterious homophonic quality of "mil" and "aire/iar" that an entirely different message comes across at point γ, namely a new signifying composite entirely foreign to the rules of the code in O. What happened is that the word *famillionaire* emerged from the telescoping of signifiers at point γ. The composition of this telescoping is freed from the code's rules for possibilities of combinatory linkage of phonemes. The fact remains that the neologism does makes sense to the listener hearing it at O. But now there is a completely new signification explicable only in terms of the creation of meaning.

What are the workings of this telescoping of signifiers that creates meaning? From the place where he speaks, the speaking subject calls up the series of signifying elements from which he must compose what he has to say. He thereby sets in motion the disruption of the signifying chain from point Δ. These are the signifying elements, sought by the subject, that will arrange themselves one after the other in a discourse according to the combinatory rules of code O. If a signifying combination not foreseen by O is produced at γ, this is because the initial signifying composite was disrupted by other signifying elements. So where do these disruptive signifying elements come from?

The shaking up of the signifying material that is called on by the subject at O gradually initiates the message at γ, since the production of meaning is due to the sliding of the two chains (signifiers and signifieds) towards each other in opposite directions. But if the subject organizes his signifying discourse by calling up the sequence of signifiers from Δ toward Δ', the message is constituted only retroactively. Indeed, the message cannot assume its meaning until the subject has called up the final signifying combination (Saussure's value of the sign). At the moment the message begins to take form at γ, other signifying elements interfere with the signifying organization that was initially intended. This initially intended signifying combination has to work together with them in order to produce, in the example we are considering, the word *familiar*. But at the same time another, parasitical signifying combination has formed to embody the word *millionaire*, which will travel along, as it were, with *familiar*, but through another circuit.

Where does this stealthy signifying organization come from, if it is not the one the subject intentionally summoned up? A smuggled-in signifying formation such as this originates in a determination that, unbeknownst to the subject, arises at β' on the graph. More precisely, this signifying combination is governed by β', which is the *metonymic object*. In our context, the metonymic object takes the form of *my millionaire*, which, for Hirsch-Hyacinth, substitutes for the object of his desire. For at that time he was a poverty-stricken lottery collector who longed to have a "millionaire" up his sleeve to help him out in his state of extreme financial need. But as much as he wished for this, there was no fulfillment of such a desire in reality, except, in a way, for the millionaire Salomon Rothschild. So it was for this reason that *my millionaire* came to take the place of the unconscious object of Hirsch-Hyacinth's desire.

My millionaire, therefore, sneaks subversively into the pre-liminary formation of the signifying chain and links up with the signifying organization of the intentional message by adding several syllables to it. Thus there are two circuits mobilized at the same time: the initial circuit $\beta \rightarrow O \rightarrow \gamma$ and the "smuggled-in" circuit $\beta \rightarrow \beta' \rightarrow \gamma$. By virtue of a partial homophony between *familiar* and *millionaire,*[1] telescoping takes place, at point γ, in a signifying condensation not anticipated by the code, one that turns out to have created meaning. Here "the message exceeds not the person we would call the messenger . . . but the support of speech (Lacan 1957–1958, seminar of November 6, 1957). Since a creation of meaning by way of signifying substitutions can take place at point γ, point γ, the locus of the message, is therefore also the locus of metaphoric substitutions. Hence this fundamental observation of Lacan's (1957–1958):

> The message, in principle, is made to be in a certain relation of distinction with the code, but there it is on the level of the signifier itself that, obviously, it is in violation of the code. . . . The witticism, because of this distinction and this difference, assumes the value of a message. The message lies in its very difference from the code. [seminar of November 6, 1957]

But if a signifying linkage not foreseen by the code is, never-theless, to assume the form of a message, the difference from the prescriptions of the code must be ratified as a message in the locus of the Other. This presupposes that the Other must,

---

1. Translator's note: The partial homophony is more striking in the original German (*familiär/Millionär*) and in French (*familière/millionnaire*), where the final syllables of each word in the pair are stressed and have exactly the same vowel-sound.

in a sense, function as what Lacan called a *third-party-Other*. This is the essential condition for a recognition that speaker and listener implicitly share in the locus of the Other, so that the new signifying compound may be accepted by both of them as a message, that is to say, as the creation of a new meaning. In other words, it is this reference to the Other that inscribes the new signifying compound in the locus of the code as a possible message.

The example of the unconscious subversion of the signifier as it operates in the joke accounts for the relationship between the creation of meaning and the metaphoric process. It also illustrates the fundamental process of the evolution of language. A language evolves to the extent that internal processes of creation of meaning arise within it through the pure play of signifying substitutions. In fact, it is in the relation of substitution of one signifier for another that the new relation of a signifier to a signified will be generated. Thus the metaphor, as Lacan (1957–1958) points out, appears as the creative force, the essential generative force, in the production of meaning:

> It is by way of metaphor, namely the play of substitution of one signifier for another, of a certain place,[2] that the possibility is created not only for development of the signifier, but also for the emergence of continually new meanings. [seminar of November 6, 1957]

In addition to explaining the joke, the graph is equally instructive with regard to the unconscious formation involved in the forgetting of names. Although this forgetting is structurally

---

2. Translator's note: "Of a certain place" refers to the resituation of a signifier from one place to another (Joël Dor, personal communication).

different from the joke, the process of its dynamic elaboration on the graph is basically the same. In forgetting, the interference of signifying elements always proceeds by way of substitution, since, insofar as something is missing in the order of discourse, something else takes its place.

Lacan (1957–1958) puts to the test of the graph Freud's (1901) famous forgetting of the name *Signorelli* as reported in *The Psychopathology of Everyday Life*. In place of the forgotten name, Freud produced a substitute series: *Botticelli*, *Boltraffio*, and, by association, the final element *Bosnia-Herzegovina*. The substitutions for the forgotten word did not appear randomly in the discourse. They were all evoked on the basis of a metonymic approximation, since they were interconnected by relations of contiguity. What is more, in these metonymic substitutions we discern the presence of what Lacan called *the ruins of the metonymic object*, or the signifying relics of the word that was forgotten/repressed. For example, the element *elli* in *Botticelli* constitutes an initial metonymic ruin of the object *Signorelli*. Similarly, we find in *Boltraffio* a relic of *Bosnia-Herzegovina*. Finally, the *Her* (Lord) of *Bosnia-Herzegovina* is metonymically linked to the *Signor* of *Signorelli* and indirectly represents the death that Freud is concerned to keep repressed.

The ruins of the metonymic object thus allow us to identify the trail of the lost signifier by means of the associative sequence:

> This is the trace, the clue that we have of the metonymic level, that allows us to find the chain of the phenomenon in the discourse, in what can be made present again in that situation that, in analysis, is called free association, insofar as this free association allows us to track the unconscious phenomenon. [Lacan 1957–1958, seminar of November 13, 1957]

The joke, forgetting names, dreams—all these formations of the unconscious have a distinctive structure in common. This structure, moreover, can be elevated to the rank of a criterion. For there is a good way to identify the origin of unconscious processes: the laws of the functioning of unconscious processes are strictly analogous to the laws of the functioning of language. This is because the formations of the unconscious are isomorphic with the mechanisms of the formation of meaning in language. In both cases, meaning is always generated by the order of signifying combinations.

The generation of meaning, as illustrated by the graph, leads directly to the question of the subject in discourse. This question can be delimited by two terms: *the saying [le dire] of the present*, and *the present of the saying*, or in another of Lacan's (1957–1958) formulas: *the discourse of the present* and *the present of the discourse*. The *saying of the present* is that which enables us to discern the presence of the speaker in his actuality as speaker. It is what speaks of itself as "I," and, along with this "I," every particle that could represent the subject in this discourse. As for the *present of the saying*, it is that which refers to whatever there is of the present moment in the discourse. Here what we are dealing with is something other than the presence of the speaker, since what is taking place on the manifest level of the message can be radically subverted by the subject's unconscious desire.

With the introduction of the dimension of desire, we must move ahead to a new level of the configuration of the graph in order to reveal its precise connections with language and the unconscious.

24

The Graph of Desire 3:
The Coupling of Desire
with the Signifier

The profound meaning of Freud's discovery of the unconscious is inherent in the problematics of the concealment of desire. Although desire is always masked in the formations of the unconscious, each such formation serves, pre-eminently, as evidence of the *recognition of desire*. But what is also involved is a *desire for recognition* in a signifying form that is immediately incomprehensible, the author having lost the key to the code of his discourse.

Recognition of desire and desire for recognition are not merely standard formulas. Under the heading of the recognition of desire we find the need of desire to make itself understood, to be recognized, even at the price of the development of a symptom or in some other appropriate form—that is, disguised. On the other hand, under the heading of desire for recognition, what slips in is the very logic of desire, the logic that dictates that desire be nothing but desire of the Other's desire and that it remain eccentric to any satisfactory solution.

Because of this fundamentally inessential structure, desire can never be fully articulated, which is not to say that it is not articulated at all. In fact, it is obliged to appear as a demand in the stream of speech. In other words, to speak is in some sense to demand, and to demand is to desire. In this connection we must now address the problem of the articulation of desire in the signifier as it is shown on the graph.

The oedipal dialectic and the paternal metaphor (see Chapters 12 and 13) enable us to be very precise about the relationship between desire and castration. We see that desire maintains a certain type of relation to the *mark*. If the subject's desire can reach a degree of maturity only after having passed through the oedipal phases, then the phallus, as the primordial object of desire, must be *marked* by something that is retained as such beyond the threat of castration. If this were not the case, the phallus could not persist as signifier of desire throughout and after the oedipal period. This characteristic, Lacan (1957–1958) adds, should be considered a sign by which the subject identifies the very dimension of castration. To cite just a few examples, the characteristic of being a sign is revealed in certain religious rituals such as circumcision, as well as in certain forms of ritualized inscriptions at the time of puberty and in the tattoos and other kinds of marks or imprintings with which the subject adorns himself.

These marks are not only signs of recognition. Beyond this, they bear witness to a specific relation to desire:

> When it comes to man, this means that the marked living being has a desire that is not without a certain intimate connection to that mark. . . . There is, perhaps right from the beginning, a gap [*béance*] in this desire that allows the mark to have its special effect. But what is certain is that there is a

very close connection between what characterizes this desire in man and the effect, the role, and the function of the
mark. [seminar of March 26, 1958]

A similar effect of the mark leads directly to the problem of
the confrontation between the signifier and desire, insofar as,
in man, this mark is the signifier *par excellence*. Lacan reduces
this relation of desire to the signifier to three successive formulas, the elements of which will occur in the construction of the
graph.

$$* \quad d \Longrightarrow \not{S} \quad \Diamond \quad o \rightleftarrows i \quad (o) \longleftarrow - - e$$

$$* \quad D \Longrightarrow O \quad \Diamond \quad d \rightleftarrows s \quad (O) \longleftarrow - - I$$

$$* \quad \Delta - - - \not{S} \quad \Diamond \quad D \rightleftarrows S \quad (\emptyset) \longleftarrow - - \Phi$$

In the first formula, the "d" represents *desire*. $\not{S}$ is the *Subject*. The symbol "o" refers to the *other* insofar as it is the counterpart of the subject, its alter ego, in the process of primary
identification with the *image* ("i") of the specular other in
the mirror stage (see Chapter 12). We also find this *other* in
Schema L, which shows the imaginary outcome of this identification in the form of the *ego* (see Chapter 18), symbolized in the
first formula by "e" as one pole of narcissistic identification. In
this sense, *the first formula shows the relationship of desire to narcissistic identification*. The direction of the arrows shows that
there is a discontinuity between "d" and "e": whether we start
from one end of the formula or the other, there is always a moment when one arrow meets another coming from the opposite
direction. (Obviously, this does not mean that there is no connection between "e" and "d." Such a connection will be explained
further on.) As for the symbol $\Diamond$ (the "awl"), it refers directly to
Schema L, reminding us that every relation of the subject to the
Other involves the ego of the subject, *o'* and its objects, *o:*

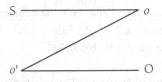

This is the meaning of what we see in this new little diamond-shaped symbol, which simply implies that everything in question here is controlled by precisely this quadratic relationship that we have always placed at the foundation of our articulation of the problem and that postulates S, that says that there is no possible S that can be conceived of or articulated, without this ternary relation: *oo'*, O, S. [Lacan 1957–1958, seminar of March 26, 1958]

The direction of the arrows in the second formula reminds us, once again, that there is a relationship that cannot be traversed all the way through, if we start out from either end, and that stops, setting out from either end, exactly at the point where the principal arrow encounters one with the opposite sign. The relationship in question here is that of *desire with speech through demand*. The symbol "D" represents the *demand*. The Other, symbolized by "O," indicates the locus of the code, the locus of speech to which the subject refers in his relationship to the locus of symbolic reference that is inevitably summoned up in the process of communication. In this second formula, "d" still represents *desire*, while "s" symbolizes the *signified*. Thus s(O) expresses *that which, in the Other, assumes the value of the signified for the subject, with the help of the signifier*. What we are dealing with, then, is what we designated as the *sign*, the *mark*. It is in relation to these signs, Lacan explains, that the identification with the *ego ideal* ("I") develops. The ego ideal is the psychic agency that forms at the time of the waning of the Oedipus complex. It has as its effect not only a process of narcissistic crystallization, but also identifications with idealized parents and collective ideals. (The ego ideal should be distinguished from the *ideal ego*, the result of a narcissistic ideal of omnipotence and heroic identifications.) In other words, this is an ideal model to which the subject tries to conform.

As for the third formula : *it expresses directly the way in which the desiring subject is brought into connection with the signifier*. The symbol Δ stands for *that which, in the subject, impels and forces him to maintain a certain relationship with the signifier S*, in that "his desire passes through demand, he utters it, and that has certain effects" (Lacan 1957–1958, seminar of March 26, 1958). This is represented by $ ◊ Δ. The symbol Φ, which stands for the *phallus*, achieves a signifying function in the Other (SØ) in a direct relation of the subject to his desire.

These three formulas constitute the dynamic infrastructure of the Graph of Desire. Basing his arguments on the most essential part of Freud's discovery of unconscious desire, Lacan uses them to try to articulate the organic relation of desire with the signifier—that is, the relation that compels the desire of the subject to assume spoken form by alienating itself in a demand addressed to the Other. When all is said and done, therefore, the subject's desire has its foundation on the level of the speech of the Other, since as Lacan has established, the subject's very speech is based on that of the Other. He demonstrates how the groundwork for this fundamental property of human desire is laid in the first experiences of satisfaction (see Chapter 20), experiences in which the child enters the universe of desire by subjecting it in speech that is backed by the signifying norms of the speech of the Other.

> For anything intersubjective to be established, the Other
> must speak, because it is the nature of speech to be the speech

of the Other, or because everything that indicates desire, primary or of the moment, takes place on what Freud calls the Other stage, this is necessary for man's satisfaction, precisely because, insofar as he is a speaking being . . . , his satisfactions have to be mediated by speech. [Lacan 1957–1958, seminar of April 9, 1958]

But in order to be based in the speech of the Other, the subject's desire must be experienced in the essential dimension of the desire of the other. It assesses the other's desire by perceiving that it bears the mark of the phallic signifier. Lacan (1957–1958) gives us a brilliant illustration of this process in his commentary on a dream analyzed by Freud, a dream Lacan on this occasion called "The Dream of the Butcher's Beautiful Wife."

In Chapter 4 of "The Interpretation of Dreams" Freud (1900) reports the manifest content of this woman's dream:

'I wanted to give a supper-party, but I had nothing in the house but a little smoked salmon. I thought I would go out and buy something, but remembered then that it was Sunday afternoon and all the shops would be shut. Next I tried to ring up some caterers, but the telephone was out of order. So I had to abandon my wish to give a supper-party.' [p. 147]

Freud's patient, who knew a bit about the psychoanalytic theory of dreams, was trying to test Freud. She expected him to state the way in which the dream bore out his thesis of the dream as wish-fulfillment, whereas, in her view, this rational and coherent dream proved that no such desire was fulfilled whatsoever.

Freud, however, offered the following explanation:

> My patient's husband, an honest and capable wholesale
> butcher, had remarked to her the day before that he was
> getting too stout and therefore intended to start on a course
> of weight-reduction. He proposed to rise early, do physical
> exercises, keep to a strict diet, and above all accept no more
> invitations to supper.—She laughingly added that her hus-
> band, at the place where he regularly lunched, had made the
> acquaintance of a painter, who had pressed him to be allowed
> to paint his portrait, as he had never seen such expressive
> features. Her husband however had replied in his blunt
> manner that he was much obliged, but he was sure that the
> painter would prefer a piece of a pretty young girl's behind
> to the whole of his face. [p. 147]

Freud continues:

> She was very much in love with her husband now and teased
> him a lot. She begged him, too, not to give her any caviare.
>   I asked her what that meant, and she explained that she
> had wished for a long time that she could have a caviare
> sandwich every morning but had grudged the expense. Of
> course her husband would have let her have it at once if she
> had asked him. But, on the contrary, she had asked him *not*
> to give her any caviare, so that she could go on teasing him
> about it. [p. 147]

At this point in the analysis, Freud makes a very useful observation:

> This explanation struck me as unconvincing. Inadequate
> reasons like this usually conceal unconfessed motives. They
> remind one of Bernheim's hypnotized patients. When one

of these carries out a post-hypnotic suggestion and is asked why he is acting in this way, instead of saying that he has no idea, he feels compelled to invent some obviously unsatisfactory reason. The same was no doubt true of my patient and the caviare. I saw that she was obliged to create an unfulfilled wish for herself in her actual life; and the dream represented this renunciation as having been put into effect. But why was it that she stood in need of an unfulfilled wish? [pp. 147–148]

After this parenthetical comment, Freud pursues the analysis.

The associations which she had so far produced had not been sufficient to interpret the dream. I pressed her for some more. After a short pause, such as would correspond to the overcoming of a resistance, she went on to tell me that the day before she had visited a woman friend of whom she confessed she felt jealous because her (my patient's) husband was constantly singing her praises. Fortunately this friend of hers is very skinny and thin and her husband admires a plumper figure. I asked her what she had talked about to her thin friend. Naturally, she replied, of that lady's wish to grow a little stouter. Her friend had enquired, too: 'When are you going to ask us to another meal? You always feed one so well.'

The meaning of the dream was now clear and I was able to say to my patient: 'It is just as though when she made this suggestion you said to yourself: "A likely thing! I'm to ask you to come and eat in my house so that you may get stout and attract my husband still more! I'd rather never give another supper-party." What the dream was saying to you was that you were unable to give any supper-parties, and it was thus fulfilling your wish not to help your friend to grow plumper. The fact that what people eat at parties makes them stout had been brought home to you by your husband's decision not to accept any more invitations to supper in the interests of his plan to reduce his weight.' All that was now lacking was some coincidence to confirm the solution. The smoked salmon in the dream had not yet been accounted for. 'How,' I asked, 'did you arrive at the salmon that came into your dream?' 'Oh,' she replied, 'smoked salmon is my friend's favorite dish.' I happen to be acquainted with the lady in question myself, and I can confirm the fact that she grudges herself salmon no less than my patient grudges herself caviare. [p. 148]

Freud concludes with an essential point about identification: "She had 'identified' herself with her friend. I believe she had in fact done this; and the circumstance of her having brought about a renounced wish in real life was evidence of this identification" (p. 149).

This dream report of Freud's is a model illustration of the dialectic of desire and demand, and even more so of the altogether stereotyped dialectic of hysteria. This is because Freud anticipates very precisely here the mechanism he would later refer to as hysterical identification. In the underlying context of the dream, the butcher's beautiful wife identifies with the friend of whom she is jealous. This identification takes place in the manner Freud describes as the perception of "a common quality shared with some other person who is not an object of the sexual instinct" (p. 108), where "in the absence of any sexual cathexis of the other person the subject may still identify with him to the extent that they have some trait in common (e.g., the wish to be loved)" (Laplanche and Pontalis 1973, p. 207).

In addition to this process of identification, we may use the case of the butcher's beautiful wife to study what is at stake in her desire. It seems that, when all is said and done, she was bent on creating for herself an *unsatisfied desire*.

Let us . . . follow Freud's thinking in the twists and turns that
it imposes on us, and not forget that in deploring them himself, from the viewpoint of an ideal of scientific discourse,
he maintains that he was forced into them by the object of
his study.

   We can then see that this object is identical to those
twists and turns, since at the first turning point of his work,
when dealing with the dream of a hysteric, he came upon
the fact that by a process of displacement, in this case
specifically by allusion to the desire of another woman, a
desire from the previous day is satisfied—a desire that is
maintained in its dominant position by a desire that is of a
quite different order, since Freud orders it as the desire to
have an unsatisfied desire. [Lacan 1958a, p. 257, translation
modified]

What can be the function of this desire to have an unsatisfied desire? This manner of fulfilling desire only confirms the
subject's fundamental subjection to the order of her desire, supported by demand. Freud's patient, apart from the dream, is very
taken with her husband, and the object of her demand is above
all *love*. And from this point of view hysterics are no different
from other subjects, except that perhaps, as Lacan (1957–1958)
notes, their problem is a bit more of a hindrance than with other
patients. The butcher's beautiful wife desires above all that her
husband should desire not to give her caviar. In other words, to
find a satisfactory solution for her love, she first has to desire
something else (the caviar), and then she has to arrange things
in such a way that she is not given this something else. She was
perfectly willing for him "not to give her any caviar so that they
could continue to love each other madly, that is, to tease each
other, to give each other endless trouble" (seminar of April 9,
1958).

This strategy of desire is very instructive. For the subject, everything is organized around the aim of creating an unsatisfied desire in the relationship to someone who, from the beginning, is precluded from the possibility of satisfying the demand in return.

> The hysterical subject is almost entirely constituted through the desire of the other. The desire that the subject here makes a point of mentioning is also the other's favorite desire, and in fact that's all she has left when she is not going to be able to give a dinner party. All she has left is smoked salmon, which indicates the other's desire and at the same time indicates that that desire can be satisfied, but only for the other. [seminar of April 9, 1958]

The Dream of the Butcher's Beautiful Wife was reviewed in order to introduce the principle of the coupling of desire with the signifier through the mediation of demand. Hysterical structure provides one of the best examples of this.

More generally, we have to consider the question at the level of need—need that can be expressed only by taking the form of a demand addressed to the other. Beyond the object of the need strictly speaking, there is something left over from the demand in which we can identify the desire of the subject through what is signified of the other. The relation of the subject to the other is fundamentally based on the effect of the phallic function, since the phallus is the signifier that marks what the other desires. Lacan (1957–1958) has revealed the essential consequence of this:

> It is precisely to the extent that the other is marked by the signifier that the subject must, can only, recognize in this, through the mediation of this other, that he too is, after all,

marked by the signifier. That is to say, there is always something that remains beyond what can be satisfied by the intermediation of this signifier or by demand. [seminar of April 9, 1958]

Lacan concludes that it is insofar as the desire of the other is barred that the subject will recognize his own desire as barred, his own unsatisfied desire. Genital desire embodies in an obvious form the status of this desire marked by the phallic signifier, or, to put it another way, barred by the mark of castration. The function of the signifier *phallus* therefore complies with the requirement that what the other desires be disguised as something marked by the signifying order, that is, as something barred. It is in this signifying specification that the coupling of desire with the signifier is located. What we have to do now is integrate this principle into the layout of the Graph of Desire in order to shed light on the relentless entanglement, in the speaking subject, of desire, the signifier, and the unconscious.

25

The "Generation" of the Graph

Establishing the Graph of Desire involves several stages. These stages do not, however, in any way correspond to developmental phases. On the contrary, Lacan (1957–1958) always considered the idea of any sort of genesis invalid. At most, what we are dealing with here is a "generation," where something of the subject is actualized in the *logical anteriority* of one phase in relation to the one that follows. These different logical phases are represented metaphorically by three schemas constituting the main successive "stages" in the setting up of the graph.

The first "stage" of the graph illustrates the relation of the subject to the signifier.

In the reality of language, this relation presupposes that something is happening over time, since all manifestations of language are organized according to a diachronic succession.

In Schema I[1] the vector $\overrightarrow{DS}$ represents this diachronic succession which is, therefore, the signifying chain. But since, in

---

1. Translator's note: The "I" here is the Roman numeral, this being the first of three graphs; it is not the letter "I" (for "Ideal") on the graph itself.

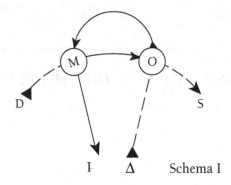

Schema I

addition, any act of language involves our being able to produce meaning, it is also necessary to assume a process of segmentation of the signifying chain that will produce the expected meaning by a certain synchrony of signifiers. This is necessary because a signifier receives its value only in opposition to all other signifiers, which is another way of saying that meaning is produced only by a retroactive effect of signifiers on their antecedents in the chain. Thus we find a second vector on this schema, $\overrightarrow{\Delta I}$, which effects a retrograde cut on chain $\overrightarrow{DS}$; we recognize this vector as the anchoring point discussed in Chapter 5. But the symbols of this schema are different from those used up to now in connection with the anchoring point. The symbol "D" stands for the *demand* that can be articulated only on the level of the signifying chain.

A signifying effect is the result of a certain intentionality on the part of the subject. Its most archaic state is the state of need; this *need*, as the point of origin of the *intentional chain*, is represented in Schema I by the symbol Δ. The subject thus enters the play of the signifying chain $\overrightarrow{DS}$ from an intention originating at the locus of need Δ that will have a certain effect on this chain. This operation is determined by the two intersections produced where vector $\overrightarrow{\Delta I}$ crosses $\overrightarrow{DS}$: O and M, the loci of the code and of the message, respectively. The subject's intention, arising from his need, must first traverse the locus of the code, since it is the code that controls access to the satisfaction of the need.

> It is insofar as the child addresses himself to a subject whom he knows to speak, whom he has seen speaking . . . that [he] must learn, very early on, that that is a path set out before him along which, essentially, the manifestations of his needs must be lowered if they are to be satisfied. [Lacan 1958–1959, seminar of November 12, 1958]

In other words, it is locus C^2 that, by prior right, will impose a structure on the need, codifying the manner in which that need can operate on the signifying chain $\overrightarrow{DS}$.

Point M is the locus where meaning is refined and completed in the retroactive play of signifiers. Thus the message takes form only *after the fact*, according to the prior specifications of the code. Under these conditions the locus of the code is precisely the locus of the Other, originally that real Other of the child's primary dependency, the mother (see Chapters 21 and 22).

This first stage of the generation of the graph may be summarized in the following major points. The subject who seeks satisfaction of a need that is as yet unformulated (Δ) must start by entering the defile of the demand. Having completed this undertaking, he comes to the other end of the intentional chain and *realizes an ideal*, symbolized on the diagram by the letter I. It is at this point that the subject's most primal identification is established as a *first signature* of what he has received from his

---

2. Translator's note: It is because the locus of the code is the locus of the Other that what is referred to as "C" in the text is represented by "O" on the diagram.

relation to the other. This final point, then, representing the imprint that demand has made on need, bears witness to the archaic apprehension of linguistic form by the subject. The very layout of Schema I is an attempt to explain this very apprehension of language. The meaning that emerges, brought about by the nature of need that absolutely must become demand in order to seek satisfaction, is unified by the circuit $\overrightarrow{MC}/\overrightarrow{CM}$ that participates in the actualization of the message. This circuit is thus distinguished by its unity (unbroken line) from the signifying discontinuity (dotted lines $\overrightarrow{DM}$ and $\overrightarrow{CS}$), and from the as yet unformulated demand (dotted line $\overrightarrow{\Delta C}$).

But this linguistic apprehension, because it is also an experience that founds the subject's apprehension of the other as such, thereby constitutes his first encounter with desire, which is first the desire of the other. This leads us to the second phase of the generating of the graph, illustrated in Schema II.

The other who can provide an answer to the appeal of the subject finds himself, by the very nature of this appeal, called upon by the subject in the form of the question "*Che vuoi?*," the "what do you want?" that Lacan (1958–1959) borrows from Cazotte's novel *Le Diable amoureux*. It is this appeal, this fundamental question insofar as it is the hold that demand has on need, that structures desire as the desire of the desire of the other. And it is the other's answer that, in turn, proves for the subject that the succession of signifiers he articulates in his demand is no longer an enigmatic proposition waiting for confirmation, but, on the contrary, that his choice of signifiers carries meaning. The meaning of the demand is dependent on the "good will"[3] of the

---

3. Translator's note: Good will is *bon vouloir*, "wanting what is good" for someone; the verb is the same as in the question *che vuoi?* (in French, *que veux-tu?*), the "what do you want?" that is addressed to the other.

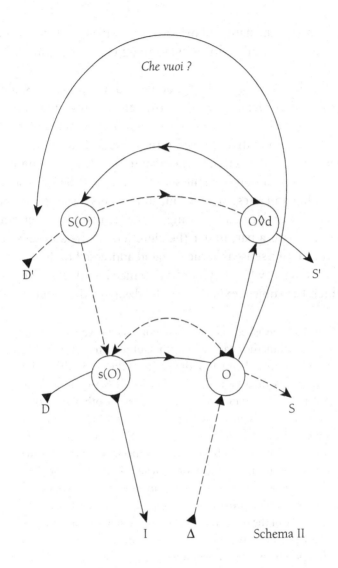

Schema II

other, who, by the nature of his response, will accord one meaning instead of another to the signifying concatenation of the appeal.

It is therefore up to the "good will" of the other to assume control in accordance with the principle of substitutability of the signifiers of demand. Since the signifiers of demand make possible a commutative choice for the other, the meaning of the demand will be delivered, in the final moment, by the commutative selection of signifiers, the selection retained, hence desired, by the other and attested by the meaning of his response. In this way, the other *fixes* the meaning of the demand by inscribing signifieds, with a bar, under the signifiers of the subject's appeal. It is in this sense that the demand addressed to the other is supported by a "what do you want?" since it ends in an answer in which the subject experiences the desire of the other.

> The question asked of the other about what he wants, in other words about the place where the subject first encounters desire, desire as being first the desire of the other, the desire thanks to which he perceives that in his being he realizes that 'beyond' on which depends whether the other will cause one or another signifier to be present (or not) in speech; that the other gives him the experience of his desire simultaneously with an essential experience, because up to this time it was in himself that the battery of signifiers was located, in which a choice could be made. But now it is in experience that this choice proves to be commutative, that it is within the scope of the other to determine whether one or the other signifier will be there. It is in experience, and on this level of experience, that two new principles are added to what was at first simply a principle of succession implying this principle of choice. We have now a principle of substitution, for—and this is essential—it is this commutativity from

which what I call the bar between signifier and signified is established for the subject. That is, between the signifier and the signified there is this coexistence, this simultaneity, that is at the same time marked by a certain impenetrability; I mean the maintaining of the difference, the distance, between the signifier and the signified: $\frac{S_1}{S}$ [Lacan 1958–1959, seminar of November 12, 1958]

The principle of commutativity is, above all, a principle of choice that can cause a given signifier to appear instead of another in the articulation of the signifying sequence of the demand. As such, it is the producer of metaphoric effects, since it is based on the property of substitution of one signifier for another. Moreover, the commutative choice of signifiers effected by the other on the level of the subject's demand is isomorphic with the fact that the utterance overlaps with the formula of the statement (even as it remains distinct from it) because of the *capture* of the subject in his discourse. Thus, for example, the articulation of the acoustic image *tymœr* necessarily calls for the *capture* of the subject's desire in the discourse in order to yield from this phonemic concatenation either the signifier associated with the idea of an organic growth (*tumeur* ["tumor"]), or the one associated with the idea of a tragic event (*tu meurs* ["you're dying"]). Such a capture also determines whether the subject will be able to articulate his unconscious desire in his speech.

In Schema II the symbol s(O) in the locus of the message (M in Schema I) represents *that which is signified from the Other*, that is, the message of the demand as its meaning is delivered by the Other according to the signifying selection that his desire has performed. The result is that, from point Δ to point s(O), the subject is never present except as a mere support of speech.

For the demand remains implicit until the moment when what is signified from the Other fixes its message. This effect is represented in Schema II by the intentional chain in the dotted line from point Δ to s(O).

Vector $\overrightarrow{D'S'}$ introduces a second "stage" in Schema II, symmetrically doubling the structure of the first one by bringing in the dimension of the unconscious. Here it is a matter of showing that the subject can sustain a demand in an articulated scansion without the support of any conscious intention. In other words, if *the unconscious is the discourse of the Other*, or if, as Lacan says, *the unconscious is structured like a language*, what this means is that the unconscious causes the discourse of the Other to continue to exist in the discourse of the Subject. In Schema II, vector $\overrightarrow{DS}$ is drawn in solid lines up to the locus of the code, O, to represent the discrete series of signifying elements that occur in the organization of the utterance; the utterance itself comes from a sequence of units of meaning governed by the rational requirement of the subject. On the other hand, the symmetrical chain $\overrightarrow{D'S'}$ is drawn in a dotted line up to point O◊d, as a metaphor for the unconscious signifying chain.

The subject's demand encounters this unconscious signifying chain at locus O◊d and thus indicates what the subject does not know, since it is precisely here that he puts his desire to the test with regard to the desire of the Other. So it is clear that *desire is necessarily separate from need* (as is shown by the symmetrical structure of the upper "stage") in questioning how matters stand with the desire of the Other at this intersection O◊d.

Starting out from the intentionality of the need, the demand summons the other at the locus of the Other (O). This is also the locus of the code from which the message of the demand will derive its meaning [s(O)]. However, beyond any satisfaction of the need, the demand is also framed as an appeal to the Other (*"che vuoi?"*). *It is in this "beyond" of the demand, extending towards the desire of the Other, that the subject's own desire O∆d is constituted.*

> From the time of its appearance, its origin, desire is revealed in this interval, this gap, that separates the articulation pure and simple, the linguistic articulation of speech, from that which marks the fact that the subject realizes something of himself there, something that has no bearing, no meaning, except in relation to this emitting of speech and that is, strictly speaking, what language calls his being.
>
> Between the transformations of demand and what has become of the demand as a result of these transformations, and, on the other hand, the urgent need for recognition by the other that we can sometimes call the need for love, there is a horizon of being for the subject; what is at stake is to know whether or not the subject can reach it. It is in this interval, in this gap, that there is situated an experience that is the experience of desire and that is first apprehended as being the experience of the desire of the other, and within which the subject must situate his own desire. His own desire, as such, cannot not situate itself elsewhere than in this space. [Lacan 1958–1959, seminar of November 12, 1958]

The subject's desire, therefore, first identifies with the imperatives of the desire of the Other, who confers on the subject's demand its entire signifying import via the return of the *signifier given by the Other, S(O)* in the locus of the message. The distance between S(O) and s(O), represented in Schema II by the vector of the dotted line $\overrightarrow{S(O)s(O)}$, shows the possibility of commutation of signifiers, that is, the occurrence of metaphoric substitutions. The locus of s(O) was previously identified (see Chapter 23) as the very locus of metaphor, because it is at this point that the signifier given by the Other S(O), governed by O◊d, can actually be substituted for the signifier of the message codified by O. The signifier of the unconscious demand ($\overrightarrow{D'S'}$) can thus telescope, in the locus of the metaphor, the signifier of the conscious demand ($\overrightarrow{DS}$) governed by the intentionality of the need. The signifying intrusion of S(O), linked with s(O) thereby creates meaning. Here we find, once again, the Saussurian algorithm of the relation of the signifier to the signified, where the bar of signification represents the distance separating the discourse of the Other as an agency of the unconscious from the discourse concretely modulated by the subject's intention. Crossing the bar, which is the principle of the metaphoric process (see Chapter 6), is therefore represented by vector $\overrightarrow{S(O)s(O)}$.

In general, this second phase of the generation of the graph of desire highlights the way the discourse of the Other prevails over the intentionality arising from need. In fact, if the discourse of the Other subverts the discourse concretely articulated by the subject's intentionality, this is because *unconscious desire comes about only through being organized in the retroactive effect of demand on need.* We can thus understand how an utterance like: *"Mais tu maries Thérèse demain!"* ["But you're marrying Therese tomorrow!"] can lead to a certain type of message in s(O) in accordance with conscious intentionality, but also, as a function of the discourse of the Other, can deliver quite another truth in the locus of the message: *"Mais tue (le) mari (de) Thérèse demain!"* ["Go on and kill Therese's husband tomorrow!"]. That is, a truth determined by the subject's unconscious desire at O◊d will promote another signifying scansion, S(O), that can cause the occurrence at s(O) of a meaning foreign to that of the message intentionally projected.

The "*che vuoi?*" thus opens up the most fundamental question that the subject encounters with regard to any fulfillment of his desire. But in order to be sustained by this "what do you want?" the process of fulfillment of desire must at first leave the subject without recourse, since the primitive presence of the desire of the Other is, as Lacan says, "opaque and obscure" to him. This opacity, aptly turned into a metaphor by the question-mark contour of the "*che vuoi?*" in Schema II (Lacan 1960, p. 313), inevitably causes distress for the subject in his relation with the desire of the other. He will try to neutralize this distress via the intermediation of the imaginary relationship of his ego with the other, as is illustrated in Schema III.

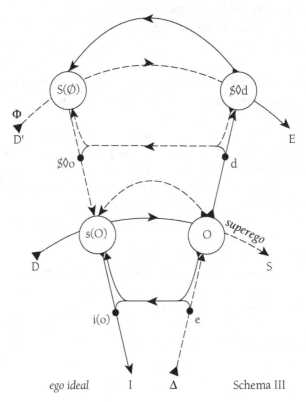

Schema III

The structure of Schema III integrates the imaginary reference points by which the subject identifies himself. The third phase of the generation of the graph completes the two earlier ones by radically situating the function of desire not only in regard to the unconscious, but also in terms of the relation of the speaking subject to the signifier. As Lacan makes clear, we must not forget that the "stages" of the graph function simultaneously in every speech act. This presupposes that something is always happening *simultaneously* at the following four points:

— Δ : the subject's intention
— O : the subject as speaking "I"
— D : the act of demanding
— d : desire

The functioning of the graph is entirely predetermined by the originary relation of the subject to the register of demand:

> The subject, in the context of demand, is, if I may put it this way, the first formless state of our subject, of the one whose conditions of existence we are trying to articulate by means of this graph. This subject is none other than the subject of need, for that is what he expresses in his demand. My whole starting-point consists in showing how this demand of the subject is, by the same token, profoundly modified by the fact that need has to pass through the defile of the signifier. [Lacan 1958–1959, seminar of November 19, 1958]

The primitive unconstituted position of the subject of need must therefore support the structural conditions imposed by the signifier. This is specified graphically in Schema III. The vector of demand $\overrightarrow{DS}$ is a solid line from D to O, while, conversely, the vector of intentionality is a broken line from D to s(O).

Now let us look at the meaning of the four new elements in Schema III: e; i(o); d; and $\$ \lozenge$ o. These four elements are arranged symmetrically in pairs on the graph. The first symmetrical pair is on vector $\overrightarrow{\Delta I}$: e and d are symmetrical in relation to O, and i(o) and $\$ \lozenge$ o are symmetrical in relation to s(O). But they are also symmetrical with each other along the two new vectors that constitute the "landings" at each level: d $\rightarrow$ $\$\lozenge$o, and e $\rightarrow$ i(o).

From the outset, the second stage of the graph must be considered the locus of the unconscious of the speaking subject. This explains, moreover, why the second stage is exactly homologous with the first. In this sense, it is clear that *it is the discourse of the Other that functions as the unconscious of the subject,* which is a brief return to the *mirror stage* (see Chapters 12 and 18) that explains the introduction of e and i(o) on the lower level of Schema III. In the mirror experience, the subject identifies himself through an image insofar as the ego (e) is constituted through an identification with an imaginary other [i(o)] who is his own image. It is this imaginary identification that contributes to the subject's primary identification, which is set up only within a dependence on the other—the mother—whose gaze sustains the establishment of this process. And so primary identification insinuates itself into a relationship with the other that is marked by very early demands, since the child's dependence on the other is based on its needs and hence on the demands that these needs evoke. Thus e and its correlative i(o) take their place on the chain of intentionality ΔI.

At this first level of Schema III we also see a "return path" from O, forming the circuit O, e, i(o), s(O). We have examined the workings of this circuit in the mechanism of the formation of the joke. Moreover, the circuit O, e, i(o), s(O) is, in a way, retrograde with respect to circuit Δ, O, s(O), I, in that it seems to function in the opposite way to primary identification I. For this reason, it is represented by a dotted line between s(O) and i(o). On the other hand, the solid line i(o) → I symbolizes the effect of the secondary influence of the ideal ego on this primary identification. This is a factor in the elevation of the primary identification to the role of the *ego ideal* (see Chapter 23). With this function, the dimension of the *superego* is introduced as the principal instrument of repression in the service of this ideal, which causes the passage into the unconscious of the discourse whose characteristic feature is the categorical imperative. The superego is therefore symbolized on the graph by a vector in dotted lines, OS.

The upper level of the graph, while homologous with the lower, is nevertheless connected to this lower level in a certain *relationship of concealment*. The concealment is all the more apparent because the locus of the unconscious process has to be in the upper level. It is represented on the graph by an opposition, vector to vector, of solid and dotted lines.

On this upper level, *desire d* is localized at a point in the trajectory between O and $◊D. In addition, it is symmetrically opposed to the *fantasy* $◊o on the other slope of the chain of intentionality. And the symbolization of vector d → $◊ implies that there is a mode of connection between desire and fantasy. Lacan examines this in a masterful way:

> What does it mean to say to a woman, "I desire you"? . . .
> Does it mean: I am prepared to acknowledge, in your being,
> as many rights as in mine if not more; to anticipate all your

needs; to consider your fulfillment? Lord, may your will be done before mine. Is that what it means? [Lacan 1958–1959, seminar of November 19, 1958]

And Lacan concludes that no one is mistaken about the meaning of this "*I desire you*," which always implicitly leads up to "*go to bed with you.*" But it is still the case—and this is where the phrase is complex—that the "I desire you" is always addressed to an object beyond the one toward which, by convention, it is precisely aimed. And experience most often shows that this aim cannot, in retrospect, be compared with what was presupposed or adumbrated in the initial "I desire you." For the object of this "I desire you" is none other than the object "around which are fixed and condensed all those enigmatic images the stream of which, for me, is called my desire. I desire you because you are the object of my desire; in other words: you are the common denominator of my desires, and God knows what desire stirs up" (seminar of November 19, 1958).

In sum, then, the *structure of fantasy* is evoked to mediate the relationship of the subject to the object of his desire, in such a way that saying "I desire you" to another always entails "I am involving you in my basic fantasy." Desire is thus in league with fantasy as the ego (e) is in league with its objects [i(o)]. Fantasy in its relation to desire is inscribed on the graph in a circuit of dotted lines to show metaphorically *the locus of the unconscious where the repressed turns around.*

So how do matters stand with the desire of a speaking subject? It is easy to see that what is unique to this desire is that it is elusive as such. Desire can be located in the signifying chain only insofar as its meaning is freed, since in this signifying chain D'E the code ($\$\lozenge D$) and the message [S($\emptyset$)] remain unknown to the speaking subject. To put it differently, only an *interpretative reconstruction* of the signifying chain articulated in the unconscious can bring forth this meaning.

> The situation of the subject on the unconscious level, as Freud explains it, is that he doesn't know what he's speaking with; the specifically signifying elements of his discourse have to be revealed to him. . . . In other words, he doesn't know the message that reaches him from the reply to his demand in the field of what he wants. [seminar of November 19, 1958]

Thus the interpretative reconstruction is what will determine, at the point of the code, *the fundamental connection that the subject maintains with his demand* $D because of the influence of desire. At the point of the message, on the other hand, the interpretative reconstruction will reveal a *defect in the signifier in the Other*, S($\emptyset$), through which the subject will experience his lack-of-being. It is around this S($\emptyset$) that the *phallus* Φ takes on its function as signifier. Indeed, the phallic signifier is the signifier that is specifically appointed to designate accurately the subject's relations with the signifier, in that it introduces the effect we have previously noted: a signifier is that which represents a subject for another signifier (see Chapter 16). "Does the subject know what he is doing when he speaks? . . . In answer to this question, Freud said: No" (Lacan 1958–1959, seminar of November 19, 1958).

In this respect, Lacan's graph achieves a remarkable synthesis of the connections that not only establish the essential basis for this question, but also confirm the irrefutability of Freud's answer. As final proof let us look at his masterful summary of the major phases of the graph:

The subject is revealed, with regard to what is veiled in language, as having this sort of familiarity, completeness, fullness in the handling of language that suggests what? Something that is precisely what I want to end with, because it's what has been missing in everything I've said in my development in three phases, so that here the energy, the depth of what I want to say to you will be complete.

On the level of the first schema, we have the innocent image. It is unconscious, to be sure, but this is an unconsciousness that wants only to pass into knowledge. . . .

On the level of the second and third phases of the schema, I've told you that we have a much more conscious use of knowledge; I mean that the subject knows how to speak and he speaks. That's what he does when he calls to the Other, and yet it is there, strictly speaking, that we find the originality of the field that Freud discovered and that he calls *unconscious*. That is, *that something that always places the subject at a certain distance from his being* and makes it impossible for that being ever to return to him, and that is why he must, *that he cannot do otherwise than attain his being in that metonymy of being in the subject that is desire.*

And why? Because on the level where the subject is involved, engaged, in speech, and thus in the relation with the Other as such, as locus of speech, *there is a signifier that is always lacking.* Why? Because it is a signifier, and *the signifier that is specifically assigned to the connection between the subject and the signifier. This signifier has a name: it is the phallus.*

Desire is the metonymy of being in the subject; the phallus is the metonymy of the subject in being. The phallus, in that it is *the signifying element subtracted from the chain of speech*, insofar as that chain engages every connection with the other, is the limiting principle that causes the subject, insofar as he is implicated in speech, to be liable to all the clinical con-

sequences that come under the complex heading of castration. [Lacan 1958–1959, seminar of November 19, 1958,
emphasis added]

And so, having completed the generation of the graph, we
have demonstrated the unfolding of the very intrapsychic process in which Freud's discovery placed the speaking subject.
Following in Freud's footsteps, Lacan has paid particular attention to articulating the intricate connections among desire, the
signifier, and the unconscious, whose effects are the key data of
psychoanalytic experience.

References

Austin, J. L. (1962). *How to Do Things with Words.* Cambridge, MA: Harvard University Press.

Bleuler, E. (1911). *Dementia Praecox oder Gruppe der Schizophrenien.* Handbuch der Psychiatrie, pp. 284–379. Leipzig: Franz Deuticke. (English trans. J. Zinkin, *Dementia Praecox or the Group of Schizophrenias.* International Universities Press, 1964.)

David-Ménard, M. (1983). *L'Hystérie entre Freud et Lacan: corps et langage en psychanalyse.* Paris: Éditions Universitaires. (English trans. Catherine Porter, *Hysteria from Freud to Lacan.* Ithaca: Cornell University Press, 1989).

Dor, J. (1981). *Suture scientifique et suture logique du sujet de l'inconscient.* Paper delivered at Fourth International Congress of Psychoanalysis, Milan, January 28–31.

———— (1982a). Scientificità de la psicanalisi? Una sovversione della cultura scientifica. *Vel , Come Comminore nel cielo—Saggi di formazione psicanalitica* 16: 149–159.

———— (1982b). Condensation et déplacement dans la structuration des langages délirants. *Psychanalyse à l'Université* 7(26):281–298.

———— (1984). *Bibliographie des Travaux de Jacques Lacan.* Paris: Inter-Éditions.

Ey, H., ed. (1966). *L'Inconscient*. Sixth Bonneval Colloquium. Paris: Desclée de Brouwer.

Freeman Sharpe, E. (1937). *Dream Analysis,* 5th ed. London: Hogarth Press, 1961.

Freud, S. (1895). A Project for a Scientific Psychology. *Standard Edition* 1:281–387.

———— (1900). The interpretation of dreams. *Standard Edition* 4/5:1–626.

———— (1901a). On dreams. *Standard Edition* 5:629–713.

———— (1901b). The psychopathology of everyday life. *Standard Edition* 6:1–289.

———— (1905a). Three essays on the theory of sexuality. *Standard Edition* 7:123–243.

———— (1905b). Jokes and their relation to the unconscious. *Standard Edition* 8:1–235.

———— (1911). Psycho-analytic notes on an autobiographical account of a case of paranoia (dementia paranoides). *Standard Edition* 12:1–83.

———— (1912). Recommendations to physicians practising psychoanalysis. *Standard Edition* 12:109–119.

———— (1915a). Instincts and their vicissitudes. *Standard Edition* 14:109–139.

———— (1915b). The unconscious. *Standard Edition* 14:159–204.

———— (1915c). Repression. *Standard Edition* 14:141–158.

———— (1918). From the history of an infantile neurosis. *Standard Edition* 17:1–122.

———— (1920). Beyond the pleasure principle. *Standard Edition* 18:1–63.

———— (1921). Group psychology and the analysis of the ego. *Standard Edition* 18:65–143.

———— (1923). The infantile genital organization. *Standard Edition* 19:141–148.

———— (1924a). Neurosis and psychosis. *Standard Edition* 19:149–153.

———— (1924b). The loss of reality in neurosis and psychosis. *Standard Edition* 19:183–190.

———— (1927). Fetishism. *Standard Edition* 21:147–158.

———— (1938a). Splitting of the ego in the process of defence. *Standard Edition* 23:271–278.

———— (1938b). An outline of psycho-analysis. *Standard Edition* 23: 139–208.

Freud, S., and Breuer, J. (1893–1895). *Studies on Hysteria. Standard Edition* 2:1–306.

Garma, A. (1954). *La Psychanalyse des rêves.* Paris: PUF. (In English: *Psychoanalysis of Dreams.* New York: Jason Aronson, 1966.)

Hegel, G. W. F. (1907). *Phenomenology of Spirit*, trans. A. V. Miller. Oxford: Clarendon Press, 1977.

Jakobson, R., and Halle, M. (1956). *Fundamentals of Language.* The Hague: Mouton.

———— (1964). Towards a linguistic typology of aphasic impairment. In Renck, O'Connor, et al., *Disorders of Language*, pp. 55–82. London: Churchill.

Jones, E. (1927). Early development of female sexuality. In *Papers on Psycho-Analysis.* London, Ballière, 5th ed. 1950.

Kress-Rosen, L. (1981). Linguistique et antilinguistique chez Lacan. *Confrontations Psychiatriques* 19:145–162.

Lacan, J. (1936/1949). The mirror stage as formative of the function of the I as revealed in psychoanalytic experience. In *Jacques Lacan. Ecrits. A Selection*, trans. A. Sheridan, pp. 1–7. New York: Norton, 1977.

———— (1948). Agressivity in Psychoanalysis. In *Jacques Lacan. Ecrits. A Selection*, trans. A. Sheridan, pp. 8–29. New York: Norton, 1977.

———— (1953a). Le Mythe individuel du névrosé. *Ornicar?* 17–18 (1979):292.

———— (1953b). The function and field of speech and language in psychoanalysis. In *Jacques Lacan. Ecrits. A Selection*, trans. A. Sheridan, pp. 30–113. New York: Norton, 1977.

———— (1953–1954). *Seminar. Book I. Freud's Papers on Technique*, ed. J.-A. Miller, trans. J. Forrester. New York: Norton, 1991.

———— (1954). Introduction au commentaire de Jean Hippolyte sur la *Verneinung* de Freud. In *Écrits*, pp. 237–322. Paris: Seuil, 1966.

———— (1954–1955). *Seminar. Book II. The Ego in Freud's Theory and in the Technique of Psychoanalysis*, ed. J.-A. Miller, trans. S. Tomaselli. New York: Norton, 1991.

———— (1955–1956). *Seminar. Book III. The Psychoses*, ed. J.-A. Miller, trans. R. Grigg. New York: Norton, 1993.

———— (1955a). The Freudian thing, or the meaning of the return to Freud in psychoanalysis. In *Jacques Lacan. Ecrits. A Selection*, trans. A. Sheridan, pp. 114–145. New York: Norton, 1977.

———— (1955b). Seminar on "The Purloined Letter." Trans. J. Mehlman. *Yale French Studies* 48 (1972):38–72.

———— (1956). Situation de la psychanalyse en 1956. In *Écrits*, pp. 459–491. Paris: Seuil, 1966.

———— (1956–1957). *Le Séminaire. Livre IV. La relation d'objet*. Paris: Seuil, 1994.

———— (1957a). The agency of the letter in the unconscious or reason since Freud. In *Jacques Lacan. Ecrits. A Selection*, trans. A. Sheridan, pp. 146–178. New York: Norton, 1977.

———— (1957b). La Psychanalyse et son enseignement. In *Écrits*, p. 34. Paris: Seuil, 1966.

———— (1957–1958). Les Formations de l'inconscient. Unpublished. Summarized in *Bulletin de Psychologie* 11(4–5):293–296; 12(2–3): 182–192; 12(4):250–256.

———— (1958a). The direction of the treatment and the principles of its power. In *Jacques Lacan. Ecrits. A Selection*, trans. A. Sheridan, pp. 226–280. New York: Norton, 1977.

———— (1958b). On a question preliminary to any possible treatment of psychosis. In *Jacques Lacan. Ecrits. A Selection*, trans. A. Sheridan, pp. 179–225. New York: Norton, 1977.

———— (1958–1959). Le Désir et son interprétation. Unpublished seminar. Summarized in *Bulletin de psychologie* 13(5):263–272; 13(6): 329–335. Some sessions published in *Ornicar?* Vols. 24–27, 1981–1983.

———— (1959). A la mémoire d'Ernest Jones: sur sa théorie du symbolisme. In *Écrits*, pp. 697–717. Paris: Seuil, 1966.

———— (1959–1960). *Seminar. Book VII. The Ethics of Psychoanalysis*, ed. J.-A. Miller, trans. D. Porter. New York: Norton, 1992.

———— (1960a). Position de l'inconscient. In *Écrits*, pp. 829–850. Paris: Seuil, 1966.

———— (1960b). The subversion of the subject and the dialectic of desire in the Freudian unconscious. In *Jacques Lacan. Ecrits. A Selection*, trans. A. Sheridan, pp. 292–325. New York: Norton, 1977.

———— (1960c). Remarque sur le rapport de Daniel Lagache: "Psychanalyse et structure de la personnalité." In *Écrits*, pp. 647–684. Paris: Seuil, 1966.

———— (1964). *Seminar. Book XI. The Four Fundamental Concepts of Psychoanalysis*, ed. J.-A. Miller, trans. A. Sheridan. New York: Norton, 1981.

———— (1966a). De nos antécédents. In *Écrits*, pp. 65–72. Paris: Seuil, 1966.

———— (1966b). Ouverture de ce recueil. In *Écrits*, pp. 9–10. Paris: Seuil, 1966.

———— (1966c). *Écrits*. Paris: Seuil.

———— (1969). Préface. In *Jacques Lacan*, by A. Lemaire, pp. 5–16. Brussels: Dessart.

———— (1972). L'Étourdit. *Scilicet* 4:5–52.

Laplanche, J., and Pontalis, J.-B., (1973). *The Language of Psycho-Analysis*. New York: Norton.

Leclaire, S. (1958). A la recherche des principes d'une psychothérapie des psychoses. *L'Évolution psychiatrique* 23(2):377–411.

Lemaire, A. (1970). *Jacques Lacan*. Brussels: Dessart.

Miller, J.-A. (1966). La suture. (Éléments de la logique du signifiant.) *Cahiers pour l'analyse*, 1/2:37–49.

Nancy, J., and Lacoue-Labarthe, P. (1992). *The Title of the Letter: A Reading of Lacan*. Albany: State University of New York Press.

Patris, M. (1981). L'identification au père. Entre l'amour et la terreur du phallus. In *La Fonction paternelle en psychopathologie*, pp. 38–47. Paris: Masson.

Piaget, J. (1970). *Structuralism*, ed. and trans. C. Maschler. New York: Harper & Row.

Safouan, M. (1968). *Le Structuralisme en psychanalyse*. Paris: Seuil.

Saussure, F. de. (1966). *Course in General Linguistics*, trans. W. Baskin. New York: McGraw-Hill.

Searle, J. (1969). *Speech Acts. An Essay on the Philosophy of Language*. Cambridge: Cambridge University Press.

Sheridan, A., trans. (1977). *Jacques Lacan. Écrits. A Selection*. New York: Norton.

Credits

The author gratefully acknowledges permission to reprint excerpts from the following:

The Seminar of Jacques Lacan. Book II: The Ego in Freud's Theory and in the Technique of Psychoanalysis by Jacques Lacan, translated by Sylvia Tomaselli. Copyright © 1978 by Editions du Seuil. English translation copyright © 1988 by Cambridge University Press. Reprinted by permission of W. W. Norton & Company, Inc.

The Seminar of Jacques Lacan. Book III: The Psychoses 1955–1956 by Jacques Lacan, translated by Russell Grigg. Copyright © 1981 by Editions de Seuil. English translation copyright © 1993 by W. W. Norton & Company, Inc. Reprinted by permission of W. W. Norton & Company, Inc.

Ecrits: A Selection by Jacques Lacan, translated by Alan Sheridan. Copyright © 1966 by Editions du Seuil. English translation copyright © 1977 by Tavistock Publications. Reprinted by permission of W. W. Norton & Company, Inc.

The Interpretation of Dreams by Sigmund Freud, translated from the German and edited by James Strachey. Published in the United States by Basic Books, Inc., 1956 by arrangement with George Allen & Unwin, Ltd. and the Hogarth Press, Ltd. Reprinted by permission of BasicBooks, a division of HarperCollins Publishers, Inc., and by Mark Paterson & Associates, on behalf of Sigmund Freud Copyrights.

Index

Contributors

Joël Dor, psychoanalyst, was a Member of the Association de Formation Psychanalytique et de Recherches Freudiennes: Espace Analytique. He was in charge of lectures and was Director of Research in the Department of Training and Research in Clinical Human Sciences at the Université Denis-Diderot, Paris VII, where he taught psychopathology and psychoanalysis. Widely published on the theory and practice of psychoanalysis, he is the author of *The Clinical Lacan* and the author/co-author of two books forthcoming from The Other Press: *Structure and Perversion* and *Lacanian Psychoanalysis: Theory and Practice.*

Judith Feher-Gurewich is a psychoanalyst practicing in Cambridge, Massachusetts, and an adjunct Associate Professor at the postdoctoral program for psychotherapy and psychoanalysis at New York University. She led the Lacan workshop at the Humanities Center at Harvard University for over ten years. Coeditor with Michel Tort of *Lacan and the New Wave in American Psychoanalysis* (Other Press, 1999), she is the author of numerous articles on psychoanalysis, the social sciences, and feminist theory. She is the Publisher of Other Press.

Susan Fairfield is a translator, editor, and practicing psychoanalyst.

Also of interest from Other Press . . .

OTHER

www.otherpress.com   toll free 877-THE OTHER (843-6843)

Printed in the United States
by Baker & Taylor Publisher Services